PRIVATIZATION IN COSTA RICA

A Multi-Dimensional Analysis

Anthony B. Chamberlain

University Press of America,® Inc.
Lanham · Boulder · New York · Toronto · Plymouth, UK

Copyright © 2007 by
University Press of America,® Inc.
4501 Forbes Boulevard
Suite 200
Lanham, Maryland 20706
UPA Acquisitions Department (301) 459-3366

Estover Road
Plymouth PL6 7PY
United Kingdom

Library of Congress Control Number: 2006907502
ISBN-13: 978-0-7618-3620-9 (paperback : alk. paper)
ISBN-10: 0-7618-3620-9 (paperback : alk. paper)

∞™ The paper used in this publication meets the minimum
requirements of American National Standard for Information
Sciences—Permanence of Paper for Printed Library Materials,
ANSI Z39.48—1984

Contents

Contents

Contents

List of Tables

Preface

This book examines the phenomenon of privatization in the context of Costa Rica. The topic is important and is vigorously debated worldwide (e.g., Vernon, 1988; Boeker, 1993; NACLA, 2003). On one hand, daily newspaper and extant literature show that in the name of economic efficiency, powerful international financial institutions press governments to sell public goods to private investors (e.g., Burtless, Lawrence, Litan, and Shapiro, 1998). On the other, popular demonstrations against such privatization have been reported—especially where the financial institutions meet. Protestors claim privatization sells off public patrimony, principally benefits private investors, and affects negatively society's poorest sectors that by definition lack resources and ready access to decision-makers (e.g., Mander and Goldsmith, 1996; Conroy, Murray and Rosset, 1996; Korten, 2001; Stiglizing, 2002; Duchrow and Hinkelammert, 2004).

Costa Rica was chosen as the venue for two reasons. First, the author is a long-time resident of the country. As director of a Latin American Studies Program in Costa Rica, he has had multiple opportunities to observe and interact with diverse sectors within the region, especially relative to the momentous economic changes that have affected it over the past 25 years. (See chapter 3.)

Second, and more importantly, Costa Rica's history and relatively well-off economic status make it unique terrain for evaluating the impact of privatization and privatization plans. These latter represent a central part of the Structural Adjustment Programs (SAPs) and free trade agreements pressed throughout Latin America by the Bretton-Woods Institutions (see chapter 1). That pressure, in turn, has given rise to a large body of literature in relation to SAPs and free trade agreements (Vargas Solís, 1990; Franco and Sojo, 1992; Aguilar Sánchez, 2003) and in relation to those programs in Costa Rica in particular (e.g., Vargas, 1991; Trejos, 1992, 1997; Valverde, 1992, 1993; A. Korten, 1997).

By way of contrast to Costa Rica's programs, their counterparts in other Central American countries are difficult to assess, since almost any large investment in Panama, Nicaragua, Honduras, El Salvador, or Guatemala is likely to produce positive results. For instance, in Nicaragua and Honduras, the second and third poorest countries in the Western Hemisphere, there is almost no room for economic regression; in these cases, it seems, "the only way is up." In Costa Rica, however, the relatively high standard of living provides a positive benchmark for assessing the impact of changes in economic policy such as those represented by widespread privatization. In Costa Rica, regression is definitely possible. Incomes can rise or drop precipitously; medical care can become more accessible or more difficult to obtain; housing and education can become more affordable, or homeless people and beggars can appear where there were none before; neighborhoods can be safer or street crime can proliferate.

With this in mind, this study examines the most recent 25 years of privatization efforts in Costa Rica. The study's argument is that the example of Central America's most economically developed and politically stable country illustrates that one-dimensional thinking about privatization of state services is misdirected. That assessment remains true whether the "one dimension" represents indiscriminate acceptance of privatization or its doctrinaire rejection.[i]

More specifically, case studies of three types of privatization attempted in Costa Rica demonstrate that in some cases privatization represents an effective response to particular historical circumstances. In other instances, however, privatization may be inappropriate. This conclusion will be based on historical investigation, the testimony of recognized authorities, analysis of arguments for and against privatization, and responses to the program in key economic sectors.

The argument is made in seven chapters. The first defines terms and provides historical perspective by examining the concept of privatization in general within the context of globalization. Chapter 2 continues by reviewing the history of Costa Rica's general political economy in order to convey Costa Rica's unique character and context. Chapter 3 connects chapters 1 and 2 by contextualizing Costa Rican privatization within the international economic crisis of the late 1970s and early 1980s, delineating Costa Rica's integration into the process of globalization Chapters 4, 5, and 6 evaluate repeated attempts to privatize many of Costa Rica's nationalized enterprises. For reasons that are explained, the chosen trio includes the Costa Rican Development Corporation (CODESA), the Costa Rican Electricity Institute (ICE) (including telecommunications), and the Costa Rican Social Security System (CCSS/INS). The chapters review the nature of each enterprise, its genesis, the reasons advanced for its privatization, and the spectrum of analysis evaluating the privatization process and results. A concluding chapter reviews the study's argument, synthesizes the evaluations provided by the case studies, draws conclusions, and makes recommendations for the future of privatization in Costa Rica.

Anthony B. Chamberlain, San Jose, Costa Rica
May 2006

---

1. The relevant literature shows that Bretton-Woods Institutions themselves have in the past distanced, and are currently distancing, themselves from unreserved support for privatization efforts. See, for instance, Chenry, Ahluwalia, Bell, Duloy, Jolly, 1974; The Economist. 1997; *Latin American Press,* 1999; Robinson, 2004; Avrigon, 2003; cf. Leipziger FPSI (Finance Private Sector & Infrastructure) Staff Survey, 2003.

Acknowledgements

Numerous people were supportive and assisted greatly in the completion of this book. Two people deserve special thanks. They are Dr. Marcus Franda and Dr. Michael Rivage-Seul. Dr. Franda served as advisor throughout the process and is professor of government and politics at the University of Maryland. Dr. Rivage-Seul, professor of religion and philosophy at Berea College, enriched the Latin American Studies Program in Costa Rica (where I work) while on an extended leave-of-absence. It is fair to say that, had it not been for the constant encouragement and valuable input of these two men, this project would not have been successful.

Chapter 1
Privatization in Context

Privatization is a controversial term (Valverde, 1992). As a central pillar of the dominant economic system, its multiple advocates speak of private ownership with great enthusiasm (cf., Burtless *et al*. 1998). Meanwhile opponents of privatization use the strongest language in rejecting an uncritical understanding of its place (cf., Mander *et al*. 1996). What is meant by privatization in the present international context requires historical perspective and a brief review of the emergence and decline of the entrepreneurial state.

Privatization in Historical Perspective

The contemporary meaning of the term "privatization" refers to something more than linking the private sector of the economy with state activities that include the commercial, financial, productive, and infrastructural. Such links have been forged for centuries. Yet, connections between the "business of government" and business itself were strengthened in the West following World War II.

Factors impelling reinforced connections of this type included the crisis of economic liberalism leading up to the Great Depression, the consequent strengthening of the labor movement world-wide, competition with international socialism, and the interest of Fordist economies in creating mass purchasing power (Duchrow, 2004). As a result, governments throughout the non-Communist world adopted for themselves a two-fold task. The first was to continue their traditional role of assisting businesses in their project of capital accumulation. The second was to offer services to citizens that would conciliate potentially conflicting social interests by increasing social welfare (Trejos, 1997). (Hereafter this type of state, with the double function just described, will be referenced using Trejos's term, the Social State.)

In the process, the state increasingly took on ownership of enterprises, especially those in which the private sector exhibited minimal interest. This often happened where there was little hope of sufficient profitability (e.g., prisons), where the volume of start-up capital exceeded the capacity of private enterprise (e.g., highway construction and hydroelectric projects), and where investment risk seemed excessively high (e.g., oil exploration, extraction and refinement). The Social State also stepped in to own and control enterprises considered especially important in terms of national security and strategic importance. Into these categories fell concerns such as energy provision, telecommunications, transportation, and agrochemicals. Finally, post-World War II Social State policy typically took control of public services such as education and health (Valverde, 1992).

The result of these tendencies was the emergence of relatively large state interference in the market place, not only among industrialized nations, but also throughout the developing world. Thus in Mexico, between 1960 and 1980, the number of state owned enterprises increased from 180 to more than 500. In Brazil, 75 percent of its state enterprises were created after 1960. In Tanzania, over a period of 15 years state-owned businesses grew from 50 to 400. Meanwhile, in Costa Rica, the country's development corporation, CODESA, set up more than 40 state enterprises (Valverde, 1992). None of this includes the numerous state institutions and programs that emerged during this same period, throughout the non-Communist world, both to assist business and to provide public services. Trejos (1997) describes such programs specific to Costa Rica:

> The most important social measures enacted during the period in question reached into every field: housing, education, health, nutrition, price-control, culture and recreation, along with the expansion of many already existing programs. In housing, programs were developed for low-income population sectors through the creation of the Institute for Social Assistance (IMAS) and through the opening of new programs in the National Institute of Housing and Urban Development (INVU) . . . (p. 38)

Import Substitution

The emphasis just noted was on markets internal to countries in the process of development. Especially during the 1960s, developing countries followed policies of "import substitution," intended to develop their own industries, as the path to development. It was noted that none of the industrialized nations had achieved their status by remaining suppliers of raw materials and agricultural products. The conviction, therefore, was that in order to industrialize, fledgling industries within the Third World needed protection. So cheaper and often higher-quality products from the developed world found themselves subjected to heavy import taxes, sometimes amounting to 100 percent of their market-determined value.

International capital in many regions of the Third World retained an important role in the development process. Both governments and multi-national firms (MNCs) were involved in direct investment that they understood would stimulate development throughout the less-developed world. Though some Third World scholars argue that this investment served more to reduce signs of economic stagnation in the investing countries than it did to stimulate development in the receiving countries, such investment did, nonetheless, contribute perceptibly to Third World economic growth. Daza and Fernandez (2004) make this point specifically in relation to import substitution policies:

Doubtless the idea behind the politics (of import substitution) was that of developing the basis of internal or sub-regional markets. Many multinational corporations took advantage of the situation to install plants and strengthen themselves within such relatively protected markets. Despite their limitations, and compared with today's politics, there resulted greater economic growth. (p. 19)

These authors claim that import substitution enjoyed relatively more success in terms of economic growth than have the policies now under discussion. The success was to last through the early 1970s.

Crisis of International Capitalism

The business-friendly Social State within the Third World fell into crisis beginning in the late 1970s. This coincided with a contemporaneous crisis of international capitalism beginning in the period from 1979 to 1982 (Valverde, 1992). Typically, the predicaments of both First and Third Worlds are attributed to the rise in the prices of fossil fuels in 1973 and again in 1979. At least three other elements must also be considered.

The Oil Crisis

The oil crisis meant a sudden increase in the price of petroleum. With the increases during the 1970s, the costs of everything made from petroleum, and transported by petroleum derivatives, also rose precipitously. This meant, for example, that the price of plastics greatly increased, as did the cost of fertilizers made from petroleum. Goods transported by fossil-fuel derivatives include virtually everything not produced purely for subsistence. Thus a near universal inflation of prices drained budgets throughout the world and made it extremely difficult for governments to sustain costly social welfare programs. Even more unviable became programs of government business ownership whose costs typically outran income, even before the rise in oil prices.

Technological Innovation and Its Limits

The crisis of international capitalism is only partially explained by the oil crisis. As Dierckxsens (2000) puts it:

> Beginning in the late 1960s and early 1970s, the world economy has shown
> symptoms of a declining growth rate. This coincided with the oil crisis that at
> first was seen as an explanation of the situation. Today almost no one attributes
> this decline in economic growth to the oil crisis (Engelhard, 1996:61). Engel-
> hard claims that this loss of dynamism is now primarily attributed to the grow-
> ing cost of innovation. These costs were apparent from the onset of the oil cri-
> sis, but intensified even as oil prices dropped again. (p. 7)

Dierckxsens here finds a major contributing factor to the period's crisis in the
development of cutting-edge technology—an advance usually associated with
the system's expansion and success. That is, the development of computer technology, super-sonic transport, robotized industrial production, cellular phones,
fax machines, and associated industrial procedures (such as just-in-time delivery)
are correctly credited as playing major roles in the development of the globalized
economy and are linked to the world-wide trends towards privatization.

Dierckxsens explains that during the 1970s such technology advanced so
rapidly that the cost of its constant replacement (in order to keep pace with competitors) eventually outran the labor costs saved by the technology itself. As a
result, profits fell, and it became expedient for owners of capital to increasingly
employ their resources outside of the strictly productive sectors of the economy
(that produced real goods), and engage in commercial activities such as currency
speculation, mergers, and buy-outs, rather than invest in new technology
(Duchrow, 2004).[1] Enterprises previously nationalized became a prime target for
such buy-outs, thus leading to the privatization of state enterprises. In the process, industrial production also fell, thus causing capitalism's crisis to deepen.

Disappearance of Socialism

A third factor, associated with the specific distress of the Social State, apart from
the attendant crisis of international capitalism, is related to the comparative success of capitalism. The reference here, is to the disappearance of international
socialism as capitalism's competitor. With that unexpected occurrence, socialism
and, by extension, programs associated with the 1930s "historic compromise"
between capitalism and socialism (e.g. Roosevelt's New Deal) were themselves
said to be discredited. In Ronald Reagan's words, government became the problem. Correlatively, private enterprise was viewed as key to successful development. Accordingly, the "crisis of capitalism" had little to do with the system itself. Instead, the crisis was attributed to the stifling of entrepreneurship engendered by the Social State itself. The system's health would be restored, it was
argued, by diminishing the social role of government, and by emphasizing its
function as facilitator of capital accumulation. The program for achieving this
end was called "structural adjustment" which involved increasingly organizing
society according to market logic of supply and demand (Valverde, 1992).

Mounting External Debt

A fourth factor contributing specifically to the Third World's part in the crisis of international capitalism was its mounting external debt. This led most directly to calls for privatization programs. The debt crisis followed on the heels of the Oil Crisis and its greatly increased profits by OPEC members and others. Much of this windfall was deposited in Western banks. Those large deposits, in turn, drove down interest rates. Interest-rate decline in turn led the banks to more aggressively seek borrowers. They offered Third World businesses and governments large loans on easy terms. Both responded enthusiastically. Accordingly, Third World debt climbed precipitously (George, 1988).

Debt increased still more as Third World banks borrowed dollars to convert the profits which multinational firms made within their respective countries. Such conversion was necessary so that those firms might share the profits with their stockholders outside of the country where profits were generated. That borrowing of dollars to convert pesos, cruzeiros, colones, lempiras, etc., all added to the debt already described.

Then during the 1980s, following the transition from military to civilian rule in many Third World countries (especially in Latin America), many of the debts resulting from private business transactions were also nationalized. The debts in question were so sizable that the debtor nations frequently defaulted even on interest payments.

> Between 1974 and 1984 alone, (Latin America's) debt grew by 620 percent (17). Since 1982 the peoples of the subcontinent have paid $100 billion in interest. During that same period, their indebtedness has risen by an additional $100 billion. Meanwhile, they have received another $100 billion in additional "aid" to finance what they owe. Already such compounding has outrun Latin America's productive capacity. Fully 45 percent of Latin America's current export earnings must be applied to financing its debt (20). Nevertheless the sum owed will reach a trillion dollars by the turn of the century (39). (Rivage-Seul, 1995, p. 46)[2]

Structural Adjustment Programs

As a result of the indebtedness just described, it became necessary to renegotiate debts through the international agencies set up for related purposes. These included most prominently the International Monetary Fund (IMF) and the World Bank. As preconditions for debt renegotiation, these agencies required the institution of Structural Adjustment Programs (SAPs), which centralized the call for

gradually advancing the privatization of government functions within indebted
countries.

> Increasingly SAPs have been accompanied by the privatization of both the real
> and the financial sectors of the economies. For most countries, particularly the
> former USSR and East European countries, it will not be inaccurate to say that
> privatization is the cornerstone of SAPs. (Haider, 1993, p.5)

The other provisions that Structural Adjustment Programs typically entail include:

> 1. Changing the state's economic function to facilitating capital transfer.
> 2. Orientation of underdeveloped political economies towards export.
> 3. Replacement of protectionist trade barriers with liberalization of all external
> markets.
> 4. Maximum privatization of state economic and social functions, especially
> education and health.
> 5. General loosening of the state's social functions.
> 6. Strengthening of the state's military and police forces.
> 7. Discrediting and dismantling organizations such as unions and cooperatives.
> 8. Stimulation of foreign investment and of the participation of foreign capital
> in all economic activities. (Hinkelammert, 1988, p.34)

Privatization and its Debate

Valverde's (1992) wide understanding of "privatization" as the process of organizing society around market principles (and whose slogan is "more market, less
state") is appropriate to the present study. Accordingly, privatization programs
will be seen as assuming three basic forms: (a) partial or total transference of a
business, institution or activity from the state to the private sector; (b) such transference where the state retains some sort of direct relation with the now-private
enterprise (such as its financing, regulation, supervision, or concession of licensing or contracts), or (c) state promotion of the privatized production of a particular good or service, and/or employing privatizing procedures within a given enterprise. In the context, "privatizing procedures" refers to the use of market
competition, or governing concepts such as efficiency or profitability. Valverde
(1992) also includes in this third form fostering and publicizing the decay of
public institutions or services so as to discredit them in the eyes of the public.
The hope here is to stimulate public petitions for the privatizing of the institution
or service in question.

As in any debate, there are two sides to the controversy about privatization
understood in the above sense. Valverde (1992) describes the two sides:

> Privatization understood as process is much more than the transference of en-
> terprises and institutions to the private sector. This is only one of the modalities

that the process adopts. In reality, it is a matter of a change in the rationality with which society organizes itself and functions.

With this process, enterprises, institutions, and services not only privatize or generate new private activities, but along with these phenomena also generate new values and concepts around social beings and the meaning of their lives. Values such as competition, productivity, individual prevalence over obstacles, all come to the fore and occupy the center of attention, and many alter values of solidarity and community organization. (p. 63)

For neo-liberals, it is important to work more to produce more. Giving priority to this concept is opposed by the opponents of such an approach who hold that the most important goals should revolve around the realization of human potential. For them, it is not as important to produce as it is to distribute what is produced. It is not sufficient merely to work; it is also necessary to recognize the right to take benefit from the fruit of one's labor and to have free time for its enjoyment. This is the general concept of life and of being human with which union and labor organizations in general confront the challenge that the process of privatization presents them at the present time. (p. 64)

Though some neo-liberals might disagree with this characterization as devaluing fair distribution, or that they would willingly deny persons the opportunity to enjoy the fruits of their labor, etc., it is probably accurate to state that the value rankings of these two sides differ substantially.

Utilizing Valverde's distinctions, and for purposes of comparison, the arguments side-by-side produce the following:

Pro-Privatization	*Against Privatization*
1. Public is counter-productive; private is good per se.	1. Private is viewed cautiously public is good per se.
2. Privatization expands consumer choice.	2. Privatized choice is premised on ability to pay, and consequently hurts society's most vulnerable.
3. Liberalizing economies eliminate state monopolies.	3. The intention behind eliminating state monopolies is to acquire cheaply the most developed and profitable state enterprises.
4. State enterprises are the principal cause of fiscal deficits.	4. Fiscal deficits result from subsidies and exemptions given private enterprise, and of the failure of businesses to pay taxes.
5. The private sector is more efficient than the public.	5. There is limited scientific data to demonstrate the comparative efficiency of the private sector.
6. Privatization obviates the intrusion of political interests as well as state bureaucracy	6. Both the public and private sectors have similar problems with special interests and with bureaucracy. The challenge is to

	eliminate them from both sectors
7. Privatization will reduce the need for governmental international loans, and consequently, external debt.	7. External debt is caused by deteriorating rates of currency exchange, by high interest rates, and by disproportionate public financial support of the private sector.
8. Privatization eliminates the need for the costly and unnecessary financing	8. Fiscal deficits are typically caused more by highly expensive and subsidizing of various activities.
9. Privatization democratizes the economy.	9. Privatization procedures usually exclude or minimize input from workers, the unemployed, children, environmentalists, etc. in the decision-making process.
10. States absorb resources, while the private sector generates growth.	10. Historically, state enterprises have generated growth. (Valverde 22-26, 1992)

The study that follows will employ these claims for and against privatization. Once again, it will examine three prominent components of Costa Rica's Social State. It will ask of each, and of the country's over-all program, whether and to what extent the privatization of those programs more coincided with the general arguments for or against privatization.

Costa Rican Privatization in Historical Perspective

Visitors to Central America, including participants in the Latin American Studies Program (LASP) with which the author works [the Council for Christian Colleges and Universities (CCCU)], are invariably struck by differences between Costa Rica and other countries of the region. Though Costa Rica belongs to the "less developed" world, it appears much more advanced than Nicaragua for example. Still showing signs of devastation from its 1972 earthquake and from its most recent Contra War during the period of Sandinista rule, Nicaragua remains one of the poorest countries in the world and reveals that status at every turn. When confronted by Nicaragua's poverty, compared with neighboring Costa Rica's relative prosperity, LASP students often ask, "Why is Costa Rica so different?"

Several years ago, a LASP student raised that question with a speaker at one of the group's conferences in Nicaragua. The speaker in question, a Sandinista sociologist, had been explaining the FSLN (Frente Sandinista de Liberación Nacional) program. He described it as embracing nationalism, a mixed economy, and satisfaction of basic necessities of all social strata.

"Why is Costa Rica different from Nicaragua?" he repeated. "That's easy. Costa Rica had its 'Sandinista Revolution' in 1948. I mean, unlike the case of Nicaragua's similar revolution in 1979, Costa Rica was allowed to bring its revolution to successful completion. For a variety of reasons, the United States did not intervene as it did in Nicaragua's case." (Fernandez, February 14, 1994)

The speaker's response was surprising to most of us. We had not been used to thinking in the terms he used. Still, what he said is arguably supported by Costa Rica's history. It did experience a revolution in 1948. That led to social reform that was spearheaded by what Costa Ricans call a "triple alliance" between labor unions, the Communist Party, and the Catholic Church. At the time, because of Soviet Russia's alliance with Western Powers and its important role in World War II, socialism and communism were not yet negatively codified as they became during the succeeding decades. Costa Rica was able to launch a program based on national sovereignty, a mixed economy, and satisfaction of basic necessities of all social strata. One of country's presidents, Daniel Oduber, even referred to the resulting arrangement as "Costa Rican socialism." Referencing the process that had been developing until his own time in office (1974-78), he said "It was necessary to nationalize many things to initiate a more integrated Costa Rican socialism, which since then has become more democratic" (Quoted in UCID, 1981, p.8).

Oduber's description is borne out by the historical incidents of what might be described as the rise and fall of the Costa Rican Social State. Until the onset of the system's crisis at the end of the 1970s, the state gave the appearance of representing the general interests, with special concern for those least able to defend themselves. Accordingly, it fixed prices to protect consumers and small producers. It placed limits on individual capital in order to guarantee sufficient "social capital" to fund programs of health, education, nutrition, housing, recreation, and culture (UCID, 1981). All of that set Costa Rica apart from its neighbors until the early 1980s.

The Costa Rican Social State

Costa Rica's system of political economy before the end of the 1970s had been based on the theory that improving the purchasing power of consumers by means of increased wages would stimulate production within local economics (Trejos, 1997). Directing that system, the state would play the central role described earlier, generally stimulating the economy, producing what the private sector was unwilling or unable to produce, providing a wide array of basic services, and acting as the employer of last resort. To achieve these ends, Costa Rica created a wide and complex social apparatus, costing 10 percent of the gross domestic product in 1950, and rising to 24 percent in 1980. During that same period, a total of 113 institutions and public enterprises were created (OFIPLAN, 1982).

Such allocation of monies and institutional creations is judged by many close observers as mostly successful. Trejos (1997) describes the characteristics of the resulting entrepreneurial state as "very advanced" (p. 34). From the 1950s on, rates of production rose by 6-7 percent. Productivity per worker increased on an average of almost 5 percent annually between 1950 and 1970 (Reuben, 1982). Among other improvements, the country added infrastructure for water, sewers, electricity, highways, bridges, and railroads (Salazar, 1986).

During this time, the prevailing economic principles made sure production was geared primarily for the internal market, which was strongly protected by the government. As a result, that market was stimulated and salaried employment grew. Likewise, the country's insertion into the Central American Common Market in 1963 extended similar protection to the entire region (Trejos, 1997). Both factors empowered Costa Rican consumers to buy more and raise their standard of living. Between 1950 and 1970, internal demand grew at an average rate of 6 percent annually (OFIPLAN, 1982).

These protectionist and regulatory policies, however, did not prevent either the country's wealth from being progressively more concentrated, or the influence of transnational companies from growing. Coffee production gravitated steadily towards the plantations of larger holders. The same dynamic was observed in sugar production. Meanwhile, foreign companies gained increasing influence over capital, technology, and patents. Their preference at this time was to negotiate with national governments, rather than with private firms (OFIPLAN, 1982).

Crisis of the Social State

As in the rest of the non-Communist world, however, the comparative success of Costa Rica's Social State fell into question at the end of the 1970s. Valverde (1992) describes the symptoms that gave rise to instability:

> The crisis manifested itself in a decline in industrial production (-4.3 percent and -7.7 percent in 1981 and 1982 respectively) and in principal agriculture exports (-8.3 percent) in 1982; in price increases (65.1 percent and 81.8 percent in 1981 and 1982); shrinking of public and private investment; increases in unemployment and underemployment; a rise in the fiscal deficit (1.734 million colones in 1978); a fall in foreign trade; mounting external debt, and sharply skewed balance of payments deficit. (p. 29)

Hoping to generate productive capital and increase employment, Costa Rican president Carazo Odio (1978-82) responded to these negative figures by increasing investment in the state's various productive sectors. His policies, however, were judged as archaic and counterproductive by important economic players. Most prominently, these included the international financial institutions that urged him to pursue a privatization plan he judged as infringing upon Costa

Rica's national sovereignty. More specifically a rift with the International Monetary Fund (IMF) led Carazo to expel its representative from the country. On March 7, 1982, the president explained his action:

> The country has exerted great efforts over the past years to adjust its life to a profoundly changed situation. We have lost help from the outside. It has been very weak and very conditioned. If we had met certain demands of the international organizations, the country would have lost its social peace. This government does not accede to orders issued from outside its borders, given that we are a sovereign people . . . This fact has obliged me to ask a representative of a certain international organization to leave the country. It simply was not acceptable to retain a functionary who wished to act as proconsul. (Cited by Valverde, 1992, p.36-37)

The result of Carazo's assertion of Costa Rica's sovereignty was a deepening of the nation's menacing economic predicament (Valverde, 1992).

The Monge administration (1982-86), which followed Carazo's, was more cooperative with the IMF. At the same time, United States' insistence that Costa Rica comply with IMF demands was softened. This more gentle approach was adopted, in part, out of consideration for the strongly negative popular reaction to structural adjustment proposals. Moreover, the country's strategic location during a time of extreme crisis in the Central American region made it imperative that Costa Rican social discontent remain under control—unlike that in Nicaragua, El Salvador, and Guatemala. The Reagan administration's military actions against the Sandinistas in Nicaragua were in full swing, as were counter-revolutionary measures against FMLN rebels in El Salvador and similar actions in Guatemala. That same conflict in a region fraught with social revolution made it imperative that Central America be able to demonstrate a "success story" as far as cooperation with the central U. S. Program of Structural Adjustment was concerned. In view of these circumstances, Costa Rica adopted a gradualist approach to the adjustment policy, rather than the "shock therapy" usually recommended and applied in other contexts (Trejos, 1997).

Despite continued popular discontent, Monge began an emergency economic stabilization program, which set the stage for later more aggressive structural adjustment measures by his successors. While still intending to protect Costa Rica's internal market in industrial and agricultural products, Monge widened commercial spaces for transnational capital, while encouraging exports. He also took steps towards restructuring Costa Rica's state apparatus along the lines that coincided with what have earlier been described as Structural Adjustment Programs (Trejos, 1997; Mora, 2004). He began the process of privatizing state businesses, institutions and public services, selling them off at cost. In these ways the president secured the support of the IMF, the World Bank, and the U.S. Agency for International Development (AID). More specifically, he signed two Letters of Intent with the IMF in 1982 and 1985.[3] In 1985 he also signed off on

Costa Rica's first Structural Adjustment Program with the World Bank, as well as several AID accords (Valverde, 1992).

President Oscar Arias Sanchez (1986-90) even more aggressively pursued the route opened by Monge. In May 1987, he clearly announced his intentions:

> It is our desire that the future of the Costa Rican economy increasingly be in the hands of the private sector. This is the goal we are working for. This does not mean strengthening the position of our nation's "haves," but rather the creation of the most promising conditions in which many might "have"...
>
>   To this end, we will try to offer productive employment opportunities to all workers who leave the Public Sector; we propose the creation of new businesses by means of fiscal and credit incentives, so that as owners themselves, these workers might offer the services that they previously offered as salaried employees. (MIDEPLAN, 1987)

Following this line of thought, President Arias further opened the country to international investment. He provided strong incentives to its export sector, and similarly encouraged the privatization of specific enterprises located under the country's umbrella Corporation for Development (CODESA). Arias also moved towards privatizing the nation's State Bank (Valverde, Manuel, Trejos and Mora, 1993). He signed two Letters of Intent with the IMF in 1987 and 1989, as well as a second Structural Adjustment Program with the World Bank in 1988 (Valverde, 1992).

The Calderon Fournier administration (1990-94) moved even faster and more insistently down the path of privatization and structural adjustment. By the time Calderon took office, the Central American crisis had largely been resolved. The Sandinistas had been voted out of office in Nicaragua. And with the fall of the Soviet Union, revolutionary groundswells throughout the world lost steam, including those in El Salvador and Guatemala. Meanwhile social protests within Costa Rica did not diminish, but intensified. This was largely due to the grassroots perception and experience that concentration on the international economy had led to nearly complete neglect of Costa Rica's internal market (Trejos, 1997). Despite this strong popular opposition, Calderon nonetheless found himself able to bypass its demands. For instance, he more completely opened the country's economy to foreign assembly plants (maquiladoras), whose only connection with the national economy remained the purchase of a few services, and the payment of workers (Trejos). Calderon also widened the "Free Zone" sector of the economy, where many of the maquiladoras had been locating since the zone's inauguration in 1981.[4]

President Calderon took as his guiding principle what was termed "economic democratization." This meant transferring to the private sector activities not considered strategic or belonging to the specific nature of the institution in question (Valverde, 1992). In following this principle, the new president was fulfilling the General Law of Concession of Public Works by Contract, which was passed by the Legislative Assembly the month Calderon took office. The law read:

> At the level of state restructuring, it is proposed to begin the work of institutional and divisional evaluation for the purposes of rationalizing institutional procedures, avoiding undue duplications, excess of personnel, irrationality in the use of human and financial resources, etc. Finally, regarding deregulation it is proposed to simplify and modernize the management and procedures of public institutions, so as not to obstruct the efforts that the most dynamic productive sectors carry out (among others, export and import procedures, tourism, banking, and construction). (Valverde, p.40)

With such goals in mind, Calderon signed two Letters of Intent with the IMF in 1991 and 1992, and "prepared the groundwork" for the signing of Costa Rica's third Structural Adjustment Program. Besides offering greater encouragement to investment on the part of international capital and to the export sector, Calderon encouraged strong application of the Labor Mobility Plan (Valverde, Manuel, Trejos, and Mora, 1993). This arrangement involved substantial layoffs in the public sector. It was met with large protests that saw public employees form a coalition with anti-privatization groups and with university students seeking increases in the country's education budget. Such pressure eventually led to the resignation of the minister of housing and to the modification of the Mobility Plan, temporarily reducing it to one of voluntary retirements (Trejos, 1997).

Case Studies of Costa Rican Privatization

Costa Rican economist Maria Eugenia Trejos (1997) suggests that discourse concerning privatization of state enterprises often unhelpfully collapses all such endeavors into a single category, "state enterprises," or even "government." Even less helpfully, within the privatization debate, all or most of a country's dysfunctions tend to be blamed on the state and public services – even without specific argument to make that case (Trejos).

In Costa Rica, such blaming and "one size fits all" solutions emerged during the crisis of the Social State at the end of the 1970s. As awareness of the state's internal deficit and external debts grew, critics frequently blamed "big government" in general and undifferentiated ways. Government spending was excessive, they argued. State intervention distorted the market. Administrative bureaucracies were bloated and inefficient. By the way of remedy, such critics broadly prescribed "privatization" as the medicine of choice (Trejos, 1997). Privatizing as much of government as possible would solve such problems, they argued.

However, as Trejos (1997) observes, such generalization ran the inevitable risks of applying a universal remedy to particular problems, instead of carefully selecting the specific antidote suited for each symptom. Problems were addressed indirectly rather than directly. Moreover, the generalizations implied in the prevailing approach obscured key differences in and between state enterprises— variations which often prove important in evaluating not only the effects of privatization, but also appropriateness of privatizing them in the first place.

Types of Privatization

With this in mind, Trejos (1997) distinguishes four basic types of state enterprises, each with different purposes, funding sources, and relations to the project of capital accumulation.

Profit-Making State Businesses

The first type of enterprise entails activities very similar to those of firms in the private sphere. Its overriding purpose here is to generate profits in competition with those firms. As will be seen below, profit-making state businesses of this type were created in Costa Rica and subsumed under the Costa Rican Development Corporation (CODESA), beginning in 1972. Under this heading, enterprises (including RECOPE, the country's petroleum refinery, and FANAL, its National Liquor Factory) were to be evaluated by market criteria of competition, efficiency, and ability to generate profits. Consequently, once "on their feet" in virtue of public funding, they might clearly be expected to be self-sufficient, though firms run by the state carried the additional burden of providing employment—in accordance with the Social State's perceived obligation of functioning as employer of last resort (Trejos, 1997). This function might make debts and deficits less objectionable, as they might with any subsidy program. This rarely proved to be the case, however, given the proximity of the crisis of '79 with the fullest unfolding of CODESA activity.

Indispensable Public Services

The second type of state enterprise signaled by Trejos (1997) embraces those that sell to the public services considered especially vital to the life of the larger community. These include water and electricity. In Costa Rica, such service is provided respectively by the Costa Rican Institute of Aqueducts and Sewers (ICAA) and by the Costa Rican Electricity Institute (ICE). Because of their importance, and because of the percentage of consumers often unable to pay the services' market costs, proponents of these enterprises argued that the services should not be judged by strict market criteria. Subsidies, it was argued, are justified. Consequently, the services' inability to generate profits or even to cover their costs was, according to this logic, warranted.

Health Care and Social Security

A third type of public enterprise provides health care and social security for citizens using as its funding source payroll deductions along with contributions from employers over the course of an employee's working career. The system is based on the recognition that salaries paid by the private sector are often insufficient to meet the needs of employees, e.g. for healthcare and retirement (Trejos, 1997). In Costa Rica, healthcare issues are covered by the Ministry of Health, while retirement is funded by the Costa Rican Social Security Depository (CCSS). The latter agency is known as the Caja (safe deposit box). As will be seen below, many health-care services prove quite amenable to privatization. Concern however is raised relative to low-wage workers and the indigent who may not be able to afford the cost of remaining in good health or of recovering health following a sickness or accident. The funding of retirement programs seems less conducive to privatization, especially in the context of Costa Rica.

Government Administration

A fourth group of state activities which have become subject to privatization is difficult even to classify as "enterprises." Here the reference is to government administration, both at the national and municipal levels. This group seems less easily and appropriately evaluated under market criteria. Sometimes the services provided are non-essential, while others may be strategic. They range from secretarial functions, accounting, and book keeping, to janitorial services and security provision. The "outsourcing" of some of these functions seems highly appropriate, while the privatization of others is questionable.

As already noted, despite such important distinctions, state businesses of all four types were increasingly privatized after 1980, and each category of socialized activity was also progressively subjected to what Trejos (1997) and others have termed "expectation creep." Herein privatization was at first justified and required because the enterprise in question was in debt. Privatization, it was argued, would lead it to balance its books. Once this had been accomplished, further privatization was required to make sure the relevant business experienced no further deficit between income and expenses; it had to balance its books now, and give evidence of sustaining such balance in the future. Third, once that goal was accomplished, further privatization was required to generate a profit. Finally, the profit generated had to be larger than the particular private firms with which the government enterprise was in competition. At each step, when government enterprises fell short, the deficiency was taken as an indication that further privatization was required.

With this dynamic and Trejos's (1997) fourfold distinctions in mind, the balance of this chapter will preview a Costa Rican public enterprise belonging to each of the categories Trejos identifies. Each enterprise type, since the end of the 1970s, has been profoundly affected by the phenomena of privatization. What follows, then, will review the nature of each venture, its origins, and the reasons advanced for its privatization. Doing so will pave the way for reviewing the effects of privatization in chapter 7.

CODESA

The Costa Rican Development Corporation (CODESA) has been the state organization most deeply affected by the privatization process (Valverde, 1993). CODESA was established in 1972. President Daniel Oduber (1974-78) explained the reasons for doing so:

> It is a question of creating within Costa Rica an institution which will develop large new industries, and which would soon attempt to transfer them to private Costa Rican investors. In this way we seek to avoid a situation in which only transnational companies would be the motor forces of industrial development in Costa Rica. Here we are talking about cement, aluminum, fishing, shipping, etc. (Valverde, p.55)

Oduber's words reflect the mentality of "import substitution," previously mentioned. Emphasis here is on heavy industry. These would be developed for eventual transferal to Costa Rican entrepreneurs, not to outsiders. In fact, by 1982, under pressure to privatize, the Costa Rican National Assembly found it necessary to pass a law specifically forbidding the sale of CODESA enterprises to foreign capital (Valverde). The purpose, then, was to avoid as much as possible control of the country's economy by outside forces.

Elsewhere, CODESA's purpose was articulated as the creation of enterprises which would take advantage of the country's natural resources, modernize its industrial orientation, and adjust it to the international market (Trejos, 1997). Thus, over the years, a large number of enterprises located themselves under the umbrella of CODESA—even beyond those itemized by Oduber. The Costa Rican Development Corporation also channeled funds towards private entrepreneurs and took on some banking functions as a result (Trejos).

ICE: Instituto Costarricense de Electricidad

The production of electrical energy, the installation of cellular telephones, and the broadcast of radio messages have all been targeted for privatization. Openings to the market, alliances with other firms from the private sector, and concessions given in that sphere, have converted portions of ICE into corporations that are essentially governed by the private sector (Trejos, 1997).

CCSS: Caja Costarricense del Seguro Social

The CCSS (or Caja) was created in 1943 in response to strong pressures by Costa Rica's labor organizations. The program was broadened and strengthened over the following years until it was eventually extended, in the 1970s, to all the country's salaried workers and to some groups without salaries.

This social security system was more than self-sufficient until the 1980s, when part of the program's surplus was transferred to the central government to alleviate debt problems generated in other government sectors and divisions. Significantly, the CCSS's funding problems were aggravated by the required early retirement of 2000 state functionaries as part of government downsizing connected with structural adjustment. As a result of such difficulties, CCSS services deteriorated precipitously during the 1980s. The number of annual consultations allowed each medical patient was limited, as were the quantities and types of medicine available under the program. Doctors were newly restricted. Hospital budgets for new equipment were cut in half in 1993. At times patients had to wait up to a year for medical consultation (Trejos, 1997).

The declining efficiency of Costa Rica's health care network resulted in calls for the system's privatization and in greater public receptivity to that idea. Accordingly, private companies integrated themselves into the system, thus creating and amplifying the number of clinics, hospitals, and consultation facilities. Pharmaceutical companies set up shop to sell unsubsidized products to the public. The Costa Rican government also awarded contracts to private companies to administer previously existing health-care clinics. Additionally, private firms and their industrial operations began employing their own medical personnel and setting up their own medical facilities to deal with the health problems of their employees (Trejos, 1997).

Such changes successfully addressed some of the country's more blatant health-care problems. Excessive waiting times for medical appointments were eliminated. Medicines and laboratory services were more easily acquired and accessed. Employers reduced the number of lost working days by setting up their own clinics and having employees' illnesses treated more expeditiously on the work site.

Still, however, several problems emerged in the newly privatized dimensions of Costa Rican health care. One was that the new services tended to be accessible only to those with capacity to pay for them. A second was that private doctors attending to work-related injuries and illnesses tended not to be properly trained for the competent rendering of such services (Trejos, 1997).[5]

State Services

During the historical period described in this study as that belonging to the Social State, government services were financed by the government itself, using its
own income. These services were often offered below cost and without the purpose of gaining financial profit. The privatization of such services led to the "expectation creep" referenced earlier. At first government services were to eliminate deficits, then to consistently balance their budgets, then to generate surplus,
then to match the achievements of analogous operations in the private sphere
(such as banks, schools and health services). Falling short of such exigencies
often indicated unacceptable levels of inefficiency, and the need for further privatization, for staff downsizing, for program reductions, for user-fee increases,
and for the reduction and elimination of subsidies (Trejos, 1997).

Review of Privatization Measures in Costa Rica

The examination of privatization's efficacy in this study makes use of a wide
meaning of the term "privatization." It is defined as the process of organizing
society around market principles. The review of privatization in Costa Rica in
the final chapter, therefore, will go beyond conclusions about the transfer of private ownership and/or management under CODESA, ICE, the CCSS, INS or
other state services. Besides addressing those specific enterprises, the final chapter will more generally assess the effects of opening Costa Rica's markets to free
market competition and of complying with the exigencies of Structural Adjustment Programs as earlier explained.

Second, in order to evaluate the effect of privatization, it is important to
note specifically the goals assigned its program by Presidents Monge, Calderon
and Arias. These goals are outlined and reviewed in chapter 7, as part of the
conclusion of this study.

---

1. For an explanation of the distinction between productive and unproductive
work, see Trejos, 117-118. Briefly, productive work (e.g., the making of automobiles) is involved in processes that increase the original value of capital.
Unproductive work (e.g., commercial transactions) does not add value to capital, but merely moves money (as in the case of interest) or already-
manufactured products from one location to another.

2. The parenthetical citations here are from Franz Hinkelammert's study produced in the Costa Rican-based Departamento Ecumenico de Investigaciones.

3. As indicated below, Letters of Intent would be signed not only by Monge,
but by his successors. These raised user fees on public services, with the intent

of generating profit. Agreements of this type would also reduce government employment by 9000 spaces. It would recommend "prudent" salary policies, keeping them constant, without regard to merit or seniority. "Prudence" also dictated elimination of automatic raises to coincide with inflation, as well as bringing collective bargaining to a halt (Valverde, 1992).

4. So-called "free zones" are industrial parks that function like states within states. They are intended to attract foreign investment in the country of location and are frequently run by their own laws which can differ markedly from legislation applicable elsewhere in the country of location. In Costa Rica, for instance, apart from salary concerns, the country's labor laws do not necessarily apply within Free Zones. Thus there is little oversight within such areas, since government inspectors are few and poorly paid. Often they end up forming special relationships with those they are supposedly inspecting. Workers (mostly young single women) are often abused. Within Free Zones, employees may be fired without explanation of due cause, and labor representatives are excluded from boards of directors. Additionally, the "host" country often owns and rents to industrial tenants their entire plant, infrastructure, and productive machinery. The result is that the companies in question can leave the country at a moment's notice, sometimes without having paid their rent or their workers (Trejos, 1997).

5. The Pavas Medical Cooperative avoided problems associated with accessibility by low-income and indigent patients by adopting a "single payer" approach. Here doctors and medical services associated with the program (general practitioners, specialists, pharmacists, radiologists, preventive specialists, etc.) received payment for services rendered, not from individual patients, but from the Costa Rican government. Thus,

> the clinic is financed completely with resources from the CCSS and from the Ministry of Health. It uses CCSS buildings and equipment. Its personnel are paid from the State budget. However, its administration is private and accordingly operates under direction outside the state system of clinics and hospitals, and outside the direction of the CCSS. (Duran *et al.*, 1991, p.180)

Chapter 2
Costa Pobre: Costa Rican
Political Economy
In Historical Context

Introduction

In stark contrast to its Central and South American neighbors, Costa Rica is often referred to as a land of peace and stability; the Switzerland of Latin America. Social and economic indicators support its exceptional reputation. Its standard of living and life expectancy are among the highest in Latin America. Illiteracy and infant mortality are extremely low. The electoral process and political life is comparable to the USA and Western Europe. And the country eliminated its army fifty years ago. All this is true despite Costa Rican being an underdeveloped country. Yet Costa Rica is presently in the midst of a deep and prolonged economic crisis and shares many of the common misfortunes of the entire region.

This chapter reviews particular historical events that have led to Costa Rica's unique social, political, and economic conditions. It posits that the participatory regime of present-day Costa Rica, where there is tolerance of legitimate opposition, is the product of unique historical developments. Its political and economic culture and structures have been established via a complex series of events and negotiations between the state and civil groups over five centuries. Chapter 2 charts the evolution of Costa Rica's political economy, emphasizing the role and development of the state and the private sector as well as public sentiments towards each. It grapples with the limitations of how much one country's historical experience and subsequent political and economic culture can be applied to others and vice versa.

Additionally, chapter 2 focuses on antecedents to Costa Rica's contemporary history, which began in the 1940s when the prevailing "liberal" state model
faltered severely and was eventually replaced by the vogue development model
of the 1960s and '70s, resulting in the state assuming primary social and economic functions. By 1980, one out of every five Costa Ricans was employed by
the state. Major public investments were being made in health, nutrition, social
welfare assistance to low-income families, social security, and other public-
sector services, including an elaborate array of public institutions to administer,
control, and conduct public as well as private sector activities. The Costa Rican
government also owned and operated numerous basic industries, including public transportation, energy production, telecommunications, insurance, banking,
cement, liquor, and fertilizer production, to mention only a few.

Analyzing how and why extensive public expenditures came to exceed revenues in Costa Rica is enhanced by this chapter's investigation. It traces the effect
of public deficits to a series of internal and external factors that produced this
nation's extended political and economic crises. This discussion sets the stage
for the chapters that follow, which will relate historical factors in Costa Rica to
current policy-making, especially those related to privatization.

Colonial Legacy in Costa Rica

Even as Costa Rica is called the Switzerland of Latin America, its early colonial experience made it the Cinderella of the Spanish colonies—scolded, taxed,
ignored, and kept imminently poor (Biesanz, 1988). Incorporated into the old-
world economic system as a colony of the Spanish mercantilist empire, Costa
Rica was initiated into a long process of underdevelopment, remnants of which
persist. But Costa Rica's emergence as a "lucky accident of nature," a sort of
"Shangri-La" (as considered by *Time Magazine's* W. Kreham while traveling
through the region in 1940), in a region abounding in dictators and corrupt mili-
taries, has its origins in the so-called "evil heritage" of Spanish colonialism
(Brignoli, 1989, p. 180).

Costa Ricans have a national holiday to celebrate the landing of Christopher
Columbus in Costa Rica during his fourth voyage in 1502. Early Spanish explo-
rations concentrated on the Caribbean coast, owing to the rugged terrain that
made access to the center of the isthmus (where most Costa Ricans live today)
extremely difficult. Impressed by the local inhabitants' generous offerings of
gold and copper ornaments, the area was named Costa Rica, or "rich coast."

Spain's search for a maritime route that might link Europe westwards with
Asia enhanced Costa Rica's strategic value. Its trans-isthmian interoceanic corri-
dor was the source of numerous conflicts with rival colonial powers. But Spain's
other principal objective in establishing colonies, "the search for wealth," was
never realized in Costa Rica. The little gold indigenous to Costa Rica (eventually

discovered centuries later) was unknown to the natives, who had acquired the artifacts that originally incited the Spaniards via trade with more distant tribes. Some, in recent times, have quipped that Costa Rica would have been more accurately named Costa Pobre, or "poor coast." One could argue that this absence of easily exploited wealth (mineral and an indigenous labor force) contributed greatly to Costa Rica's long-term peace and stability. Far from Costa Rica, mineral- and labor-rich Guatemala became Spain's administrative center for post-Mayan Central America. (In 2005, Guatemala is still dealing with the serious fallout of 40 years of violent civil conflict that ravaged that country during the second half of the last century.)

Frustrations over Costa Rica's lack of mineral resources were exacerbated by an indigenous political geography that was complex and confusing to early colonizers. Unlike the Inca and Aztec empires, which were centers of Spanish viceroyalties (and later the republics of Peru and Mexico), dozens of chiefdoms or "naciones" in the Intermediate Area had to be conquered one by one.

Typically, under the Spanish repartimiento system, indigenous peoples were obliged to work as serfs for a given number of days each year. In exchange for Christianity and protection, neighboring Guatemala, El Salvador, and Nicaragua used this already-present labor force to produce exotic tropical crops for export to European markets. But the system largely failed in Costa Rica because the sparse indigenous population (which had been heavily reduced by newly introduced viruses) retreated to ever more remote areas, out of the reach of the colonizers. Sixteenth century conquistadors actually pillaged the crops of the locals before the few Europeans who remained gave in to farming for themselves. The first settlers had little choice but to work small plots of land that they could manage with their own physical labor—a situation unheard of in almost any other part of Latin America. In a 1719 report to the Captaincy General of Guatemala, Costa Rica's governor stated that even he had to personally "perform this labor, for if he didn't he would perish" (Busey, 1962, p. 40). Thus, there emerged a pattern of small family farms, wherein land was distributed quite evenly among the settler yeomanry. What was produced was for subsistence consumption. The little that was exported was sold officially to other Spanish colonies in the Americas, though some was sold illegally to English smugglers along the Caribbean (Brenes, Castillo, 1978).

For lack of precious metals and any significant native labor force to produce export commodities, Costa Rica was dismissed by the Spanish empire as a minor frontier province. Sixty-two years after Columbus's landing, Costa Rica's first permanent settlement was established in the meseta central and became the headquarters for the colonial province. The distances and difficulties in traveling between provincial capitals created politically fragmented territories that were isolated and contributed to the development of separate traditions and characters within each of the Crown's possessions. These geophysical realities and the accompanying sociological phenomena were the antecedents to what later became the five independent republics of present day Central America. Not only did they impede the establishment of a single isthmus-wide state, they continue to hinder efforts at regional cooperation.

Over three centuries, barely a few thousand Spaniards actually settled permanently in Costa Rica. Their advanced material culture brought about deep structural changes, far out of proportion to the number of Spanish who immigrated. Imposed was a new geopolitical system wherein heterogeneous native groups gave way to a Hispanic American society. The new Costa Ricans were at once poor and neglected but proud, self-reliant, and accustomed to a considerable degree of freedom. Multiple pre-independence accounts refer to the formation of a national consciousness of individualistic small landowners, scornful of both ecclesiastical and political authority, isolated and uninvolved with commerce, as the foundation of Costa Rican democracy. Theirs was an impoverished but egalitarian "rural democracy" (Monge, 1977). Despite differing social backgrounds, which, along with race, formed the basis for Spanish American social, political, and economic organization, "Costa Rica retained a much greater degree of racial and economic homogeneity than its neighbors . . . Social inequities in Costa Rica were never great enough to let one class or race completely dominate others to the detriment of the majority of the populace" (Booth and Walker, 1989, p. 25).

During colonial times, the very conditions that kept Costa Rica poor were also instrumental in isolating it from the raging disputes that were common in other colonies. As the state had few resources, Costa Ricans became accustomed to seeking solutions to their problems without governmental assistance. Those who early governed Costa Rica held to a practical "liberalism," some founded on idealistic convictions, but most often merchants and businessmen looked suspiciously upon state intervention. There are, however, cases in which the colonial state government fulfilled entrepreneurial roles that would much later became commonly accepted, even expected, by Costa Ricans. One such example is the Costa Rican Tobacco Factory (an estanco). Beginning in 1766, it functioned as a state entity and oversaw the planting, harvesting, and exportation of tobacco. It was viewed as a decisive instrument in the economy of the country, particularly important for the vigorous growth of the newly-founded city of San José. At its height, between 1787 and 1792, this state industry was the monopoly supplier to the entire Audience of Guatemala. Eventually, however, it was hampered by shortages of labor, prohibitions by Spain on sales to external markets, competition from other colonies, isolation, and expenses in overland transport. As a result, the tobacco industry was in decline by the end of the colonial era. Capital accumulated from this state monopoly did, however, sustain the central government of Costa Rica until the middle of the next century and provided funds for public works. In this sense, the tobacco industry (and to some extent cocoa) can be seen as the precursor of the agro-export economy consolidated in Costa Rica after its independence (Hall, 1985). It also served as an important early experience of state ownership of an enterprise more typically controlled privately.

It is not the case that colonial Costa Rica developed and experienced what could be considered genuine democracy. A status hierarchy—based on race, noble lineage, and wealth—created a national aristocracy and governance through municipal councils (cabildos), reserved primarily for its members. Leaders of what later became political parties emerged from this political class and shaped early Costa Rica's liberal and conservative camps (Melendez, 1985). Nevertheless, the fact that Costa Rica could not exploit the "hacienda" system (which flourished in the rest of Latin America), and that it avoided the kinds of violent conflicts and wars that exploded throughout most of colonial Latin America, did contribute to later opportunities for genuine democratic reforms and set the stage for the acquisition of independence without bloodshed (Booth, 1989).

Emerging Nation: Independence to the First Republic

Costa Rica emerged from the colonial period as an exception to the region's political, economic and social norms. If the seeds of its uniqueness were planted during that period, they took root in the nineteenth century. While the rest of the isthmus was ravaged by civil wars, Costa Rica entered the new century as the most backward and least important of Spain's five Kingdom of Guatemala provinces (today's five Central American countries). When the other four were elevated to "intendencia" status in 1786 (which allowed each to maintain its own local government), Costa Rica remained a "gobernación" (which made Costa Rica accountable to Nicaraguan authorities). But Costa Rica also experienced the greatest relative peace throughout the 1800s of any developing state in the region. "The political intrigues that characterized other Spanish American colonies were largely absent, and the inherent conflict found elsewhere between prosperous but politically powerless creoles on the one hand and Spanish officials on the other never applied in Costa Rica" (Rinehart, 1984, p. 16). Costa Rica's destiny as a nation-state, however, was clearly tied to the actions taken by her neighbors.

At the turn of the century European capital was being used primarily to finance the industrial revolution at home. Spanish ties were weakening, while British, German, and U.S. interests were growing in Latin America. The British, in particular, were active along the east coasts of Nicaragua, Costa Rica, and what is today Panama. Nevertheless, Costa Rica demonstrated loyalty to the Spanish crown through 1821. Costa Rican volunteers, for example, fought beside Spanish troops in the suppression of a British-supported Nicaraguan revolution in 1811. The break came in October of 1821, when the news arrived in Costa Rica that Mexico had been granted independence, and that the Captaincy General of Guatemala (which held Spanish jurisdiction over Costa Rica) had in turn proclaimed independence for all of Central America. The leaders of Costa Rica's four principal "Meseta" councils were forced to reexamine their position. By December, a representative junta had placed in service a provisional constitution, in order for the dust to settle, before determining their course of action. Mexico, Guatemala, and Nicaragua were embroiled in heated conflicts over who would dominate Costa Rica, and each of Costa Rica's four main towns was claiming independent rights. By May 1822, Mexico's Agustín de Iturbide was demanding that Costa Rica submit to his newly proclaimed Mexican empire. In response, the majority of Costa Rica's leaders registered agreement to the union with imperial Mexico. In the process, however, there surfaced two factions within Costa Rica that were to clash for many years to come. The conservative, aristocratic leadership in Cartago and Heredia strongly favored the imperial ties. Progressive republicans in Alajuela and San José, on the other hand, who held rising liberal sentiments, were promoting either union with the rest of Central America or an independent Costa Rica with a republican form of government.

Imperialist sympathizers from Cartago and Heredia marched on San José in December 1822 in an effort to force compliance in joining Mexico. This civil war was short lived; several hundred republicans from the other two major towns met and defeated them in the outskirts of Ochomogo. By March 1823 the victorious republicans had moved the capital to San José and formally declared Costa Rica's independence from Spain. Fear of intervention by Mexico moved the provincial congress to apply for union with Colombia at the same time. These events coincided with an unexpected Mexican revolution that overthrew Iturbide, thereby reducing the threat from Mexico and freeing the young Costa Rican Congress to join the United Provinces of Central American in August 1823. Commonly referred to as the Central American Federation, which Nicaragua, El Salvador, Honduras, and Guatemala had formed in previous months, its federal constitution provided that each province elects its own chief executive. Accordingly, the provincial leader was empowered to deal with internal matters while foreign affairs were relegated to the jurisdiction of the federation president. Costa Rica's elected provincial congress chose Juan Mora Fernández as "jefe supremo" in 1824.

When compared to the chaos, coups, and civil war that engulfed its neighbors during the succeeding ten years, Costa Rica's experience was peaceful. Mora worked hard at unifying the new nation that according to Carlos Monge (1976) behaved more like "a group of villages separated by narrow regionalisms" (p. 192). Each of the four principal towns retained its own municipal council and its own specific political, economic and social orientation. In efforts to dispel divisiveness and build unity, Mora offered rewards to any group that would develop roads, ports, or other means of promoting province-wide commerce and industry. Mora was reelected in 1829, the year Costa Rica's first newspaper was circulated.

Replacing Mora, Juan Rafael de Gallegos was elected in 1833. Under his leadership, an early example of a Costa Rican compromise was codified in the

Law of Movement. The law stipulated that the seat of government was to be rotated among the four key towns every four years. When this agreement failed to quell persistent conflicts, de Gallegos resigned in despair in 1835 (Rinehart, 1984).

Braulio Carrillo Colina, who replaced de Gallegos, undid the rotating capital compromise and firmly established San José as the provincial seat. He did so by putting down multiple assaults on San José by a Cartago, Heredia, and Alajuela alliance intent on unseating the government there. In the process Carillo earned a reputation as a heavy-handed dictator. Attempts to unseat him via the elections of 1838 were foiled when Carrillo, although he lost the election, disregarded the constitution and seized control of the state by force. Three years later he abolished the constitution altogether and declared himself dictator for life. These same authoritarian methods eventually led to Carillo's exile in 1842.

Even so, Carrillo, a forceful liberal, is credited with important accomplishments. Carillo replaced the archaic Spanish legal system with a new legal code, organized an efficient and honest public and financial administration, decreed that ownership of municipal lands be given to the "private" farmers who worked them, and paid in full the debts incurred from membership in the Central America Federation. Similarly, on the issues of national unity and integration, whose measures continued to be viewed by conservatives as imposed on the country by liberals, Carrillo soundly overrode opponents. Costa Rica's withdrawal from the federation and subsequent proclamation of its sovereignty in 1838 (formal independence was declared in 1848) had less to do with a loss of the dream for a united Central America (which persists to this day) than it did with the violent unrest between the Federation's northern provinces. Furthermore, the Federation had proven an economic drain and a constraint on Costa Rica's desire to pursue the coffee markets that were developing in Europe. This is the area where Carrillo's policies had, arguably, the most lasting repercussions for Costa Rica's political, economic, and social development.

Coffee drinking was a growing fad in Europe, particularly in Britain and Germany, and Carrillo saw an economic opening for Costa Rica. He required even poor people to cultivate coffee plants near their homes in exchange for tax exemptions and land grants. It turns out that the temperature, soil, rainfall and altitude in the meseta central, where most of Costa Rica's population was concentrated, is the ideal combination for growing high-quality coffee. Furthermore, processed coffee had the advantage of being an imperishable commodity that held up well during the slow trek by ox cart and ship. And since there was little competition from rival crops or indigenous groups over land rights (problems that plagued its neighbors), Costa Rica was in an excellent position, early on, to reap profits from supplying Europe's growing demand for coffee. Coffee became the economic engine for Costa Rica's development. By the late 1800s the majority of Costa Rica's population was dedicated to some aspect of the production and exportation of coffee. For the next fifty years coffee was virtually Costa

Rica's only export. Today the ox cart that carried coffee over the mountains to port is Costa Rica's most prominent national symbol—since it put Costa Rica on the map economically.

Costa Rica actually gained political independence before it consolidated the colonial economy typical of other Latin American settlements. While Guatemala and El Salvador were perpetuating hierarchical/oligarchical systems, and Honduran and Nicaraguan populations were divided and struggling with foreign interventions, Costa Rica became the first country in the region to establish a neocolonial export economy. This development derived precisely from the fact that Costa Rica had been sparsely populated, underdeveloped, and had experimented early on with forms of representative government, unhampered by the social and economic problems associated with large indigenous and slave populations, common in much of the rest of the region. Both the colonial economy of desarrollo hacia afuera (externally oriented development) and the neocolonial export economy were based on the notion that the export of a few valuable primary products would finance the import of necessary raw materials and desired manufactured items. As long as a country's profits from exports exceeded its population's demands for things from abroad, a bright future seemed assured.

Indeed, Costa Rica benefited tremendously from its early entry into the coffee export business, and this economic arrangement fueled a period of economic growth and progress that took Costa Rica into the twentieth century (González Flores, 1974). Not only did the upper class minority grow rich, but as a national enterprise coffee raised the living standard for the majority of the population and bridged the political and economic interests of both groups (Facio, 1972). At the same time, the success of coffee revealed the weakness of Costa Rica's agro-export economy. Coffee's proliferation stifled the production of grains, root crops, fruit, vegetables, and livestock—all of which grew well in the meseta central. As early as the mid-eighteen hundreds, Costa Rica began importing large quantities of beans, maize, rice, wheat, animal fats, and vegetable oils in response to several subsistence crises. Local manufacturing dwindled to the point where all but liquor was manufactured entirely by artisans, of which seamstresses were the largest group. England supplied the machinery for the coffee industry as well as most consumer goods. Erratic fluctuations in the price of coffee (and later bananas) contributed greatly to periods of economic crisis in Costa Rica, and Carrillo's legacy helped make and break political futures as well.

Like most of the early export sectors in Latin America, the production of coffee remained largely in the hands of nationals (Sunkel and Paz, 1973). The modest capital that a few prominent colonial families were able to accumulate from the earlier, pre-coffee, production of cocoa and tobacco, and from gold mining, was invested in the new export industry. Further subsides came in the form of advance payments from European and American importing houses. Local exporters and millers used these funds to supply credit to small producers whose harvests they handled. An elite class developed within the industry among

the largest producers and exporters. Land ownership became increasingly concentrated and a new class of landless agricultural workers appeared. These elite
"cafetaleros," however, never established a monopoly over the cultivation of the
crop. And although two-thirds of the rural population came to be employed on
the larger plantations as laborers, they nevertheless realized wages superior to
the typical income of small independent farmers. The families that dominated
the industry served as wholesalers for the numerous small-scale coffee farmers.
These dominant producers and exporters became known as the "Coffee Barons,"
Their wealth, while modest when compared to the elite of other Latin American
countries, provided the political clout that shaped their century and greatly influenced the next.

Member of these elite families were influenced by the theories of economic
liberalism then popular in Europe. And though often in competition with each
other, most were persuaded by the laissez-faire capitalism practiced in England
and "identified the well-being of the nation as a whole with their ability to pursue
their commercial activities unimpeded by government interference" (Rinehart,
1984, p.21). Whether from within the government or indirectly, via influence,
the coffee families sought to minimize taxes and bolster policies that encouraged
the coffee trade and enriched its owners. But equally influential in the evolving
role of the Coffee Barons was the interdependence among the rural classes that
had developed in Costa Rica during the colonial period, which reinforced egalitarian social values. Because members of the peasant class were neither slaves
nor passive exploited employees, their employers found it necessary to establish
a set of symbolic and normative social mechanisms, by which peasants would be
persuaded to work (Vega Carballo, 1982). The new Coffee Barons, converted
from the old social and political aristocracy, continued to dominate national politics but were growing increasingly preoccupied with organizing the electoral
process without aggravating too severely the important working class. Evidence
of their concerns included early post-independence experiments with expanded
popular suffrage, direct elections, and the establishment of electoral rolls. Participation in mid-century ritualistic, secondary elections rose from two percent of
the population to more than eleven percent by the century's turn.

During this period, the ideological fervor between liberals and conservatives
that was a source of tremendous division and violence in the northern provinces
was much less significant in Costa Rica. Instead, individualistic, independent
farmers, large and small, bonded around their own commercial interests and ad-
vocacy of minimal government intrusion. But commonality of interests did not
mean harmony or equality. In actuality, "political affiliation ... had more to do
with family (rather than class) traditions, regional associations, and the personality of candidates offering themselves for office than it did with a political
agenda" (Rinehart, 1984, p. 20). Property and literacy qualifications granted
voting privileges and political influence to a restricted minority (10 percent of
adults) with strikingly similar interests. Most elections were non-competitive and

indirect. The liberal, secular consensus among the coffee oligarchy and the small size of the eligible electorate made political parties unnecessary. Politicians simply formed temporary informal networks (Peeler, 1985). Yet enemies and allies were almost always from families among the same coffee-growing elite who fought for political office and military rank among themselves. This intense competition among members of the most powerful families degenerated at times into electoral fraud and violence, evidenced in events that extend from the Carrillo dictatorship (when the Coffee Barons surfaced), to the Guardia dynasty (that first subdued the coffee elite).

The perpetrators of Carrillo's military overthrow in 1842, who restored the personal freedoms that had been lost, were themselves executed only months later when attempting to force the Federation's reestablishment. After several years of instability, a congress of Coffee Barons named José María Castro Madriz president in 1847. He became Costa Rica's first chief executive to hold this title, in recognition of the nation's full sovereignty. Castro Madriz severed ties with what remained of the northern Federation and declared Costa Rica's formal independence in 1848. His government pushed numerous reforms, of which development of education and the confirmation of freedom of expression and association were primary goals. But when the president abolished the army, a coalition of coffee elite and displaced military officers forced his resignation. His replacement, coffee baron Juan Rafael Mora Porras, proved less responsible for the temporary cessation of internal hostilities than was a series of events from outside the country (which would be the case little more than a hundred years later).

Mora Porras's government was on the verge of collapse (he dissolved a rebellious congress and was using fraudulent means in an attempt to win a second term as president), when one of the most transcendent events in Central American history – more so, according to some authorities, than independence – transpired (Biesanz, 1988). Fueled by the region's liberal-conservative struggles, competing foreign business interests (including those of American Cornelius Vanderbilt) and a strong belief in "Manifest Destiny," American adventurer William Walker led a band of mercenaries in overthrowing Nicaragua's conservative ruler and eventually took the presidency for himself in 1855. His expansionist plans to eventually hand all of Central America over to his supporters as part of a "Confederacy of Southern American States" included an attack on Costa Rica in 1856. Advised of the impending invasion, Costa Rican President Mora, with the authorization of the Legislative Assembly, succeeded in raising an army of 9,000 men. Costa Ricans from every social class enthusiastically volunteered. In the ensuing engagements, Mora Porras lost half of his army, but forced Walker's retreat. Subsequent attempts by Walker to take other parts Central America failed and he was eventually executed in Honduras. His misadventure in Costa Rica, however, inadvertently united Costa Ricans, who demonstrated for the first time a sense of nationalism that transcended entrenched localist interests and feuds that were so predominant in prior decades. One of the most highly honored national heroes in Costa Rica today is Juan Santamaría, who gave his life in a courageous act while battling against Walker.

The victory against Walker, which made Mora Porras a war hero, unraveled only months later. Rival coffee baron José María Montealegre declared himself president, and, with the support of troops loyal to his family, ousted Mora Porras. A failed counter-coup, attempted by Mora Porras a year later, resulted in his execution. The Montealegre family, backed by the same army that had helped them overthrow Mora Porras, controlled the Costa Rica government during the next ten years through puppet presidents. Elections were held, but they were indirect and campaigns were noncompetitive. The divisive squabbling of the Coffee Barons persisted.

Privatization in Mid-19th Century Costa Rica

During the presidency of Juan Rafael Mora (1849-59), a concerted effort was made on the part of the cafetaleros (coffee planters) to privatize peasant agrarian holdings in Costa Rica's Central Valley (Castro, 2004). A coffee baron himself, Mora saw coffee as the product that would bring prosperity to his class, and by that class's line of reasoning, to the entire country. Thus, Mora fostered an alliance between the great landowners and rising middle class planters to expropriate land from poor farmers in San Jose, Alajuela, Heredia, and Cartago (Costa Rica's primary cities then and today in the wealthiest and most heavily populated Central Valley), in order to expand the coffee estates. The poorer farmers found themselves at a distinct disadvantage in the proceedings, since they were mostly disqualified from legislative office. Thus they were excluded from the decision-making process that would deprive them of access to the communal lands they depended upon for their livelihoods. To qualify for municipal and state office, one had to be at least 21 years old, own real estate worth 300 pesos or have half that as an annual income, be up to date with tax obligations, and be able to read and write. Few campesinos (peasants) met that profile (Castro).

Accordingly, farmers depending on communal lands were informed that they needed land titles to continue the labor that had been based on usufruct rights (Castro, 2004). In the absence of proper papers and of the financial resources to buy the lands in question, the small farmers found the lands they had been cultivating – in many cases for more than a generation – enclosed and incorporated into the estates of those with greater material means. Better-off farmers who could muster the money to buy parcels of the formerly communal lands did so. However, following the struggle against the U.S. filibuster, William Walker (1856-1857), many of these farmers were left without means to repay the debts they had incurred while their lands stood idle during their service to their country (Castro). These too watched helplessly as their lands were enclosed and integrated into coffee estates belonging to the barons.

The effects of the entire process of land privatization are well described in the following petition registered by Costa Rican peasants in 1858:

> In agreement no. 100 of 2 March 1858 of the Ministry of the Interior, the government decreed that 25 plots of that land should be remeasured, and enclosed, appraised, and put in the hands of the Intendent General for auction, with the goal of investing the proceeds in the piping system that currently provides water to the capital. On these plots today you will find the best coffee haciendas of Señores Montealegre, Le Lacheur, Hubbe, etc., etc. and previously Don Juan Rafael Mora, under whose administration the matter of these lands was decided. As in all things relating to the public good, despite the beneficent desires that generally animate the Head of State, these kinds of machinations leading to the private benefit can always be seen. This is what has happened in the matter which we bring before you today, since . . . San José with the immense benefit of piped water, and the landowners with their valuable haciendas on the outskirts of the most important population center of the Republic, have acquired uncommon advantages, but the People of Pavas have been reduced to indigence for they have nowhere to provide for themselves, and have no access even to firewood. What an adverse effect has come of reducing to private domain the common lands on which we live. (p. 39-40)

These words indicate the process by which privatization occurred. First the land in question was expropriated from the Commons by the state (whose head had a vested interest in the proceedings). Second, the land was then auctioned to the highest bidder—invariably one of the large landowners of the day. Third, the monies were invested by the state in improving the holdings for the new owners by, for example, adding a water provision system, which even further increased the advantage of the hacienda owners over their peasant competition. Predictably, the end result was the private benefit of the few while the majority, who depended on the produce and also on the firewood from the formerly communal lands, suffered

The First Republic

The reign of the Coffee Barons was finally broken by General Tomás Guardia Gutiérrez. His iron-fisted rule helped make possible what is often referred to as "the First Republic." Guardia led a 1870 coup against Jesús de Jiménez Zamora, who had been placed in office for a second time by the Montealegre family. Jiménez had asserted his authority by removing two generals in an effort to submit opposing factions within the army to civilian control. Guardia's disgruntled military faction prevailed, and, after a short period of controlling the government through his own puppet administrator, Guardia was elected president under the provisions of a new constitution (the eighth since 1825). The new constitution, which remained in force until 1949, provided for a College of electors who were selected by popular vote, and who in turn elected the president.

Charles Ameringer (1982) argues that infighting among the elite families actually produced the Guardia military dictatorship (1870-1882), whose rule would succeed in curtailing the power of the Coffee Barons. But by the time the army became politicized, Costa Rica had already developed a habit of civilian rule. This, more than likely, contributed to the eventual fall the Guardia dynasty and the birth of the First Republic, discussed below (Booth, 1989). What is known for sure, however, is that from 1824 to the election of 1889 (which marks the beginning of the First Republic), eleven of Costa Rica's 24 presidents were indirectly elected, seven took power by force, and six were appointed "temporary" presidents for brief periods. The average presidency lasted only 2.4 years, and Costa Rica was under military rule over half the time. The generals who became president were almost all coffee aristocrats.

A populist, Guardia fulfilled his pledge to end the dominance of the politically powerful coffee families. He did so by forcing into exile large numbers of the old liberal establishment, silencing open political debate, banning political associations, and levying stiff taxes on personal wealth. Guardia even ignored his own constitution, which forbade successive terms, when at the conclusion of his first term he dismissed the legitimately elected president and ruled as dictator until his death in 1882. Though despised by the Coffee Barons, Guardia endeared himself to the majority of the population by confiscating large land holdings and distributing them among landless farm laborers. Tax revenues helped finance the extension of education and the expansion of public works. But it was Guardia's pursuit of a railroad linking the Central Valley to the Atlantic coast that had the greatest long term political, economic, and social effects on Costa Rica.

The project's principal aim was to facilitate the transport of increasing volumes of coffee to port for export. To accomplish the task, Guardia contracted John Meiggs, an American, whose nephew, Minor Keith, eventually completed the railroad. In the process, however, Costa Rica exacted tremendous debts relative to its size (an obligation under which Costa Rica strained well into the next century). Keith agreed at one point to fund the national debt, in exchange for huge concession of undeveloped lands along the tracks approaching the Atlantic seaboard. With capital from U.S. investors, Keith established banana plantations on his new land, which proved ideal for growing the exotic crop that was gaining rapid popularity abroad. By 1890, bananas began to rival coffee as the most significant factor in Costa Rica's economy.

Since the coffee oligarchy was concerned about the possible competition for power if a second agrarian bourgeoisie were to form, they did not invest in bananas, and the eastern province, where banana plantations flourished, remained for many decades an isolated enclave (Vega Carballo, 1975). This situation was aggravated by the fact that Costa Rican laborers largely refused to become part of railroad or banana work crews. Keith, therefore, brought significant numbers of Italians and Chinese into Costa Rica. It was black immigrants from Jamaica, however, who eventually saw the railroad to completion and provided the ongoing labor for the burgeoning banana industry in the Atlantic province of Limón. These English-speaking Jamaicans retain their unique social institutions and cultural identity to this day. In fact, their employment outside of Limón was officially denied until 1952 when they were first given citizenship. It is worth noting that these immigrant laborers were responsible for the first united expressions of discontent in the work place: a strike by the Chinese in 1874; a mutiny by Jamaicans in 1879; and a major strike by Italians in 1888. Native Costa Rican laborers emulated this new form of expression in a telegraph strike in 1883. Similar acts became much more prevalent in the twentieth century.

Railroads and bananas shifted the focus of Costa Rican trade from European to U.S. markets. They also contributed greatly to the ongoing transformation of Costa Rica's traditional subsistence economy to that of a specialized commercial-agricultural "dessert economy" whose well-being was increasingly dependent on much larger, foreign economies. Profits from trade in coffee and bananas did finance impressive advances in Costa Rican society under the multiple leaders of the nineteenth century. These included expanding public education, transportation, and civil liberties, improved urban sanitation and health care, abolishing capital punishment, establishing a postal system, and trade incentives that increased agricultural production. Furthermore, John Booth (1989) identifies three types of organizations sponsored by the period governments that reinforced social differentiation but also deepened the government's involvement in protecting wider social interests. The first were mandatory guilds for doctors, lawyers, miners, ox drovers, boatman and dockworkers. The second were mutual-aid societies that were deemed necessary as the economy became increasingly subject to international market forces, and the workforce had to cope with unemployment for the first time. The third, multitrade self-help guilds, were important political springboard organizations that mobilized their artisan and laborer memberships.

During this hundred-year period in which Costa Rica had become independent and unified as a nation, its population began to develop an appetite for government services. But the period also retained and reinforced a Costa Rican distaste for governmental expectations from them. Indeed, most shifts in presidential power had come as a result of attempts by different administrations to impose requirements upon the governed, usually in the form of direct taxation or conscription. In the long run, though, "the presence of a significant number of independent small farmers, the weakening of the socioeconomic elite soon after independence, relative racial homogeneity, the rural labor shortage, and the expansion of popular education combined to create an environment in which democracy could take root" (Booth, 1989, p. 26). These democratic roots find expression during Costa Rica's First Republic, and provide important insights into Costa Rica's present.

Liberal Ascendancy of the First Republic

In 1989, U.S. President George H. W. Bush traveled to Costa Rica to join in the celebration of 100 years of democracy and the inauguration of San José's Democracy Plaza. This important event points back to the shift from "patriarchal" to "liberal" democracy and specifically to the presidential election of 1889. That election has come to mark the birth date of competitive democracy and a party system in Costa Rica, known as the First Republic. It is often called the Liberal Republic because, in that same election, the Guardia dynasty of 20 years gave way to a group of young liberals (whose political lineage traced back to the old pre-Guardia liberal establishment), who came to govern Costa Rica over most of the next fifty years. People today remember them as the "generation of '89." They believed in the separation of church and state, that the state should dominate, and that formal education was the key to solving the nation's problems. Electoral fraud, violence, and an elitist grip on the political process did not disappear during this period, but all classes were increasingly influenced by a free press, and the awareness of their ability to effect the choice of political leaders and public policy was ingrained. "During this era, democratic elections, honest civilian public administration, and peaceful transfers of power gradually became standard practices" (Biesanz, 1988, p. 170). From the election of 1889 to the present the constitutional electoral process has been interrupted on only two occasions: one, during the First Republic, was the Tinoco brothers' dictatorship, which fell due to popular pressures after only two years; the second coincided with a short-lived civil war and the advent of the Second Republic.

That Costa Rica became a democratic country during this period of liberal ascendancy—gradually employing classic liberal-representative means to organize and transfer political power—is well established. Important factors contributing to their employment and adoption are given expression during the First Republic. But this period has also been interpreted as the turning point, where Costa Rica's agro-export economy ceased to generate continuous growth and prosperity. By relying almost exclusively on only two exports, but unable to produce sufficient quantities to dominate the international markets in either, Costa Rica was particularly vulnerable to economic depression and ecological hazards. Reduced prices from glutted coffee markets, devastating banana diseases, and world depression in 1929 found Costa Rica's export production unable to keep pace with the demands of its rapidly growing population. (During the last half of the nineteenth century Costa Rica's population tripled, nearly a quarter of whom were European immigrants.) The subsistence economy of frontier colonization no longer provided a sufficient buffer between production and pricing short falls and its respective dependent labor force (Saeez, 1969). Costa Rica's economy maintained this basic structure throughout the First Republic, however. Attempts to lessen the country's dependence on world markets, by adopting internally-oriented development policies, are the primary distinction between the economy of the First and Second Republics. Antecedents to this change, from an external to an internal orientation, are an important part of the subject matter of the First Republic.

The touchstone for Costa Rican democracy—the election of 1889 that marked the founding of the First Republic—was hardly exemplary. Not even 10 percent of the population had the franchise. Indeed, as Election Day approached, sitting President Bernardo Soto Alfaro imposed his own candidate, since by then it was clear he had insufficient votes to win. What is unique, however, is that, for the first time, large numbers of Costa Rican laborers marched angrily with sticks and machetes on San José, in what has been called a popular democratic revolt, to insist on their right to choose the president. Equally unique, Soto withdrew his candidate and ensured constitutional transfer of government by ceding power to the rightly elected opposition candidate, José Joaquín Rodríguez Zeledón. This was a first for Costa Rica.

Soto was unique in a number of other important ways. He had succeeded to the presidency of his brother-in-law, Próspero Fernández Oreamuno, who died in office in 1885. Fernández Oreamuno was the brother-in-law of the dictator, Guardia, who died in office in 1882. All three men saw themselves as progressives. Fernández Oreamuno enacted laws that severely restricted the role for the church as a social institution. But it was Soto who oversaw the institution of Costa Rica's remarkably free, secular, and compulsory public school system (via his minister of finance, education and commerce, Mauro Fernández), which particularly affected Costa Rica's future. Illiteracy fell from 90 percent to 40 percent in Fernández's lifetime. This alone greatly increased the number of eligible voters (since literacy remained the primary criteria) and also provided new avenues of access for many more to became involved in political activities (Booth, 1989). Soto also broke ranks with the past in the 1889 election by allowing full freedom of the press, open debates between the candidates, and an honest tabulation of the vote.

The election of 1889 was a key event in the process of establishing Costa Rica's modern political parties. The Catholic Union Party (Partido Unión Católica—PUC), considered Costa Rica's first genuine political party, was organized in 1891, in reaction against Rodríguez who was elected in 1889. The PUC's aim was to defend the interests of the church through the electoral process, but its criticism was focused on the inequities fostered by the ruling elite's laissez-faire economic system (Rinehart, 1984). The PUC did not prevail against the liberal movement, which, while fragmenting on several occasions, dominated Costa Rican politics for the next five decades. But like the short-lived reformist party of the 1920s (whose platform was Social Christian Antioligarchical), the PUC was instrumental in shaping a new social agenda for the country. The latter also created openings for future cooperation between the Catholic Church and working-class unions. The Communist Party of Costa Rica (PCCR), founded in 1931, also played an important role in organizing voters and was especially important in events that paved the way to the Second Republic. Other challengers to the liberals' stronghold revolved around personalistic campaigns whose party names rarely endured beyond a single election. There was, however, a rapid expansion of non-partisan organizations and associations that during this period made increasing demands on the political system.

The liberal leaders of the "generation of '89" produced several largely personalistic factions of their own that operated under various political party titles and alternated in presiding over the events of the First Republic; the Republican Party (PR), the National Republican Party (PRN), and the National Union Party (PUN) dominated the period. Although, these parties were held together more by patronage than by program, and the power of the old political families – broken under Guardia—was reasserted, their presidents did preside over important political and social reforms that included the First National Election Consul (Consejo Nacional de Elecciones, 1925), the secret ballot (1928), and the institution of direct popular elections of public officials where even peasant leaders (gamonales) were voted into municipal posts (1914). As a result, new names from outside of the old aristocracy began to appear on congressional rolls as prosperous small farmers began to emerge as a force in local government. Despite these changes, executive manipulation of elections and fraud did not disappear (Booth 1989).

By creating access to public office beyond the aristocracy, more and more of the general public became interested in active political participation. Political Sociologist José Luis Vega Carballo (1990) argues in *Political Parties, Party System and Democracy in Costa Rica,* that the rising popular acceptance of a centralized state, in conjunction with the civil oligarchy's consent to parties as an acceptable means of carrying out presidential successions, guaranteed sufficient resources and power for the parties to function. Furthermore, the increasing autonomy between the political-institutional power of the state and the parties vying for office coalesced to assure that entrepreneurs were unable to control completely political structures or the economy. The space in the system that was opened for the middle and lower classes to channel their demands resulted in a much more integrated social structure in Costa Rica than in other parts of Latin America. Although voter participation in national elections throughout the First Republic never rose much above 15 percent, the nature of Costa Rica's evolving democratic structure was truly exceptional in that there existed opposition that was active at regular intervals but was not forcibly excluded, persecuted, or terrorized. Even if opposing parties often represented similar platforms, they nevertheless lent a democratic character to elections and to the formal political game wherein political parties become deeply imbedded institutions (Vega Carballo, 1990).

For Vega Carballo (1990):

> Costa Rica's democratic regime was possible only because the social forces that formed the state opted for the political party as the instrument by which to organize their participation. Thereby they created strong, dominant parties that would have an impact across generations. Only in this way was it possible to consolidate a strong political center that was moderate, pluralistic, open, and capable of discouraging informal, often explosive, intervention from outside the political system. (p. 203)

Accordingly, even as the late nineteenth-century Guardia dictatorship was partially the result of squabbling among the coffee elite, so too his heavy-handed rule led the same "cafetaleros" to promote political parties, elections, and expanded suffrage to protect their political influence from future dictators (Aguilar Bulgarelli, 1974). Since open domination from above had become largely unacceptable and counter-productive in Costa Rica's context of "relative class equality," democratic mechanisms proved helpful in the coffee-growers retention of power, especially in the early twentieth century. Vega Carballo (1990) contends that the "rules of the game" that developed during this period helped maintain and validate the established order and formed a false sense of egalitarian ideology. Complete with an accommodating rhetoric, the ruling class pretended to obtain consensus. In this way it took credit for the minimal recourse to violence and force, yet kept in check the conduct of the subordinated classes.

Attributing the above to a premeditated orchestration by a united national bourgeoisie would be inaccurate. John A. Booth believes such a view is too simplistic given the political divisions between anticlerical liberals and pro-Catholic elements that developed into various personalistic faction (1989). The conclusion drawn from the present study is that the similarities of the deepest interest among the bourgeois factions outweighed their differences and was the greatest force in the evolution of the illusionary egalitarian consensus. In a fascinating parallel with the two dominant contemporary political parties (from 1948 to the present), Vega Carballo (1990) states that the Republican party (PR) of the First Republic "successfully alternated in power with an opposition so similar to it that its competitors did not dare present viable alternatives" (p. 206). The PR, backed by strong popular support, took on the causes of special interest groups within civil society, approving reforms, but only after carefully calculating their adoption so as to assure the PR's control (Vega Carballo, 1990).

The perpetuation of this notion has led activist scholars like Julio Quan (LASP lecture, September 26, 1992) to conclude that "Costa Ricans are the most repressed of all Central Americans," and a recent Mexican ambassador to Costa Rica to comment that "Costa Rica is on the verge of political chaos because its two major political parties represent 'the same oligarchy'" (Mesoamérica, 1997,

p. 10). Neither view, however, supports the notion of a self-conscious and united effort by the elite. Both, instead, recognize that liberal-representative devices were eventually adopted, the consequence of elite factions struggling for influence in an increasingly complex social, political and economic landscape where dictatorial rule was distrusted and experience with the violently repressive means so common in neighboring countries, was counterproductive and minimal (Booth, 1989).

Understanding the First Republic and its impact on the circumstances of present-day Costa Rica would be incomplete without (a) making reference to a number of incidents that underline the futility of separating politics from its economic context, and (b) providing examples of the crucial impact that external forces had on the small, vulnerable country of Costa Rica during this era. President Alfredo González Flores is a prime example. González Flores came to power in 1914 after Costa Rica's first experience with direct presidential elections, although he was not even a candidate. (Two of the three legitimate candidates withdrew and the third, of which the majority disapproved, was ruled ineligible.) His appointment by congress was a bloodless compromise, the likes of which became well known in Costa Rica.[1]

González Flores came into office professing commitment to a progressive social platform. Shortly after his inauguration, however, González Flores became aware of the seriousness and precarious nature of a Costa Rican economic crisis that previous governments had been loath to admit or tackle. Over-production of coffee by Brazil, already the world's leading producer, had greatly reduced prices worldwide and in turn caused a prolonged depression in Costa Rica from 1897 to 1907 (Cardoso, 1973). Hopes of a strong and prolonged recovery were finally dashed when the outbreak of World War One virtually closed European markets. Faced with declining revenues, capital flight, and heavy debts, the president declined the pursuit of foreign loans (common practice under previous administrations) and instead reduced public expenditures (including salaries), raised export taxes, and laid plans for a progressive income tax in a context where previous taxes had been indirect and regressive and therefore negligible (Biesanz, 1988). These measures actually greatly expanded the government's role in the economy. Historical records indicate that legislators of the day understood that the actions of González Flores were necessary. Nevertheless, he quickly lost favor among the agro-elite, businessmen, and the masses, liberal and conservative alike, and was attacked as a radical (Rinehart, 1984). Plans to reverse his policies via the elections of 1918 proved unnecessary when his Minister of War, Federico Tinoco, allied with his brother Joaquín, seized power by a popularly-supported military coup in 1917.

The Tinocos were unable to turn around the desperate economic situation and came under early, heavy criticism. The situation was exacerbated by the USA's withdrawal of diplomatic recognition of Costa Rica, consistent with President Wilson's policy of breaking relations with governments that had come to office by unconstitutional means. Wilson prevented Costa Rica's delegates from signing the Versailles Treaty and threatened intervention. These actions damaged trade relations between the two countries at a time least affordable by Costa Rica.

Tinoco responded to the mounting dissent by clamping down on civil liberties and jailing or exiling political critics. Tinoco's troops even fired on the U.S. consulate where some demonstrators had taken refuge. Popular protests swelled. "Costa Ricans might have tolerated an ineffective government, but they repudiated one that overtly mistreated them and restricted liberties they had come to expect" (Biesanz, 1988, p. 22). Costa Ricans were now rejecting the military solution and trumpeting again their preference for civilian, constitutional governance.

Eventually, the assassination of Tinoco's brother Joaquín and an imminent counter-coup orchestrated by Costa Rican exiles in Nicaragua persuaded Tinoco to flee to Europe. Turning over the government to his vice president was unacceptable to the U.S.A., which insisted on new elections and a return to constitutional government. In a show of force, the U.S.S. Denver docked off of Costa Rica's Atlantic coast. Subsequently, Tinoco's vice president resigned and the U.S.A. accepted one of González Flores's vice presidents as an appropriate legal representative. Regular elections resumed again in 1920 (Rinehart, 1984).

The policies pursued by González Flores were predicated on the internal and external political and economic realities of his time. But the consequences for his administration and the country's political system were dire and set a dangerous precedent. While the Tinoco dictatorship was short-lived and Costa Rica's democratic tradition has only been interrupted on one other occasion (the civil war of 1948), numerous parallels with the González Flores scenario may be drawn from descriptions of successive Costa Rican administrations that help expose Costa Rica's contemporary predicament.

Postwar leaders strove to bring order and peace to the country's tattered economy and dubious international relations, within a testy domestic environment. In pursuit of those ends, they employed orthodox recipes. For the most part the state's role was limited to foreign affairs, maintenance of law and order, building schools and roads, and collecting import and export duties. This last function constituted the government's principal source of revenue. But a perpetuation of the status quo also meant a hands-off approach to addressing the degenerating material conditions of the underprivileged majority. This "business-as-usual" approach occurred in the context of the world depression of 1929. Costa Rica was even more severely affected by this crisis than the depression at the turn of the century. Coffee prices and banana production fell to record lows. Neither industry recovered to pre-depression levels until well after the Second World War (Hall, 1985). "Costa Rican liberalism became in a way a victim of its own success in providing an effective educational system, which over a period of four decades had produced political awareness among a relatively large middle class that now not only saw the possibility of social and economic change but also desired it" (Rienhart, 1984, p. 35).

In the wake of acute poverty and rapid population growth, members of the urban middle class, workers, and farmers became organized in demanding that the government address disparities in the distribution of wealth, lack of health facilities, malnutrition, poor housing, unemployment, and inadequate transportation. Discontent was increasingly focused on the land-owning liberal elite and their functionaries, who held office through their patronage. Protest movements—with nationalist and unionist with socialist orientations—spawned cooperatives, labor unions, and professional and trade associations, as well as school and community organizations. Demands by this mobilized citizenry proliferated. The Communist Party of Costa Rica (PCCR) founded in 1931, became deeply involved in electoral activity. It also established the Costa Rican Workers' Confederation (CTCR) that soon became the nation's predominant labor organizer. The CTCR mounted a huge strike among banana plantation workers in 1934. Although the strike was resolved through negotiations, workers developed a taste for the tangible fruits obtainable as a result of their organized efforts. The successful strike also threatened the upper classes and some middle-class conservatives (Vega Carballo, 1990), which raised race tensions by giving the predominately black banana workers a voice (Rinehart, 1984). The occupation of Nicaragua by U.S. Marines during this same period fed both the rhetoric of the leftist intelligentsia (which stirred Costa Rican workers) and raised fears among Costa Rica's privileged.

Faced with pressures to find solutions to old problems from increasingly militant organized labor and a stalled economy, Ricardo Jiménez Oreamuno, one of the last active survivors of the old liberal "generation of '89," and now president for a third non-consecutive term, dabbled with new forms of direct government intervention. By 1936 coffee production was being regulated, in an effort to stabilize descending prices. A minimum wage was enacted and a state-owned insurance monopoly was established that offered subsidized coverage. Jiménez Oreamuno even repossessed 250,000 acres of unused land from the United Fruit Company and had it distributed to landless farmers in 125 acre plots (Rinehart, 1984).

Opposition within the Republican Party to Jiménez Oreamuno's concessions had forced the party to improve its abilities to mobilize voters. The old-money coffee families were especially concerned about popular demands for further social reform and heavier taxation of the wealthy. With their backing, the conservative, anti-labor, pro-Nazi Republican, León Cortés Castro, won the presidency in 1936. Cortés Castro ousted the party's old guard, suppressed the civil liberties of political opponents, dissolved the Electoral Tribunal (disallowing congressmen to be seated), and initiated a crackdown on communist political and union-organizing activities. Since Cortés Castro could not constitutionally succeed himself, he determined to select a pliable candidate for his newly renamed

National Republican Party (PRN), who might maintain the status quo until he could legitimately claim the presidency again, four years later. Cortés Castro chose the charismatic pediatrician Rafael Angel Calderón Guardia, who won the presidency in 1940 for the PRN with 90 percent of the votes. The Communist Party took the other 10 percent, despite fraud and limitations on the part of the PRN, and increased its representation in both the Congress and some municipalities. Nevertheless, the solid victory of the PRN and confidence in the perpetuation of Cortés Castro's policies under Calderón, provided a sense of calm among the victors. The calm, however, proved short-lived.

While both Cortés Castro and Calderón were of a different stripe than the traditional liberal elite, their own differences, which would be played out in the tumultuous 1940s, hobbled the monolithic elite. For the first time since Guardia in the 1870s, several distinct voices became politically articulate in Costa Rica. Periodic events also saw the role of government expand greatly, along with new attempts at industrialization and economic diversification. At a major turning point in Costa Rican history, these forces divided the nation and climaxed in a civil war that brought the First Republic to an end, giving birth to the Second Republic.

Calderón showed himself early on to be independent-minded as he pursued a policy course radically different from his predecessors. Whether this was the result of genuine Social Christian ideological convictions or merely pragmatic checks on the growing influence of the communists, is debatable (Biesanz, 1988 and Rinehart, 1984). Whatever the case, Calderón made deep social and economic reforms a primary goal of his administration. Depression-impoverished workers and portions of the growing middle class rallied behind Calderón's call for reforms. But long-time party loyalists among the elite were alienated. Calderón instituted social security and health insurance programs, and enacted a comprehensive labor code that guaranteed a minimal wage, collective bargaining, workers' rights to organize and strike, and protection against arbitrary dismissal. Squatters were also provided legal means to acquire titles to lands that they were cultivating. In addition, the University of Costa Rica was founded and served middle class groups. In order to push these reforms through congress, Calderón entered into a strategic but precarious alliance with the communist party (palatable to typically anticommunist Costa Ricans only because of their war-time alliance with the Soviet Union) and the Catholic Church's small but important Acción Católica (Catholic Action), an activist organization dedicated to promoting religious education and relief for the poor.

In the course of Calderón's term, most members of the bourgeoisie (the traditional enemies of redistributional reforms and communism) defected from Calderón's National Republican Party and joined the disgruntled Cortés Castro, who ran for president again in 1944 under his newly formed Partido Democrático (Democratic Party). Two other groups, Acción Demócrata (Democratic Action) and Centro para el Estudio de Problemas Nacionales—CEPN (Center for the

Study of National Problems)—proved important in the alliances formed during this period. Made up of several hundred young middle- and upper-class professionals, law students, and white-collar workers, members of these groups referred to themselves as "modern liberals" (to distinguish themselves from the old traditional liberals of the previous era). They were inspired by Roosevelt's New Deal in the U.S.A. and his Good Neighbor Policy for Latin America. Their common aim was the reorganization of government institutions that would foster economic and social development via democratic means. For them this implied modern political parties based on distinctive ideologies that offered related policy packages rather than parties and programs based on cults of personality, an accusation increasingly made of both Calderón's PRN and Cortés's PD. They also sought to defend electoral purity (highly valued though rarely experienced) and to eliminate corruption.

These groups came to oppose Calderón's administration, but were unable to coordinate their efforts sufficiently to prevail over the well-organized Bloque de la Victoria (Victory Bloc) of the PRN and the communists. As a result, Calderón's handpicked successor won the 1944 presidential election by a margin of two to one. But the traditional political center that the Republican Party had controlled over the past 50 years (under its various names) began to fracture, and its strength in civil society was greatly weakened. The instability of the center meant that the Republican Party was losing its balancing and integrating role in the political system. Instead, its inability to manage social tensions via the legitimate tools of the state led to the use of deceptive measures and police coercion to maintain the new reforms and to take the 1944 election (Vega Carballo, 1990).

Calderón was, nevertheless, still viewed by many working-class Costa Ricans as the one president who was genuinely concerned for their welfare. And Calderón was intent on taking the presidency again for himself in the 1948 elections. Picado's term became one long electoral campaign, with Calderón basically continuing to pull the strings behind the scenes (Biesanz, 1988). But equally determined to defeat Calderón were members of the oligarchy, conservative anti-Communists idealistic reformers, and ambitious activists. Among these were the two personalist parties of Cortés and Otilio Ulate. Together they formed a coalition called "La Oposición" (The Opposition), with that one goal in mind. An important element within this coalition was the newly formed Partido Social Demócrata—PSD (Social Democratic Party)—that resulted from the merger of the practically-oriented Acción Demócrata and the ideologically-driven CEPN. Modeled after the prewar European social democratic parties, the PSD advocated a systematic approach to progressive reform, which for Costa Rica meant a drastic overhaul of the present political system if meaningful changes in other areas were to be achieved. José Figueres Ferrer was given a leadership position in the new party when he returned to Costa Rica a hero after being exiled by the previous administration for delivering an anti-Cortés Castro radio speech at the prodding of Democratic Action's leaders. While exiled in México, Figueres formed an alliance with dissident leaders from other parts of Central America and the Caribbean (known as the Caribbean Legion) to aid each other in toppling regional dictators, establishing democracy, promoting social justice, and pursuing a new Central American Union. Figueres favored armed rebellion and was convinced that the incumbents would not permit the opposition an electoral victory. Figueres, therefore, actively plotted the government's overthrow by stockpiling arms and training multinational insurgents with funds from the Guatemala Government. In so doing Figueres disregarded Costa Rica's time-honored tradition of seeking resolution through peaceful compromise, and the nation's historic isolationism, and has proved the nemesis of those in power (Biesanz, 1988).

The economic slump that followed World War Two was a source of tension in Costa Rica that expressed itself in numerous incidents of antigovernment demonstrations, strikes, partisan violence, and even several attempted coups. Cold War obsessions in the U.S.A. that filtered into Costa Rica made the Calderón/Picado alliance with the communists a growing political liability, in a context where the communist's militia was proving increasingly valuable for their government that was under almost constant attack. "Under pressure, the government became more arbitrary in its actions. Acknowledged and suspected opponents of the regime were periodically rounded up by police and held for questioning, in disregard of the law. Although most were soon released, some were forced into exile" (Rinehart, 1984, p. 42). But when several civilians were killed by government forces during a protest over irregularities in the 1946 congressional election, the multiple opposition forces were outraged and became more concerned than ever about the possibilities of an honest election in 1948. This became the central issue of their campaign and, in 1947, a massive general strike was staged (known as the Huelga de los Brazos Caídos—Strike of the Fallen Arms) that successfully brought the country to a virtual standstill. Ulate, who had been chosen by the Opposition to run against Calderón (Cortés had died in 1946), was demanding a guarantee of open elections in return for an end to the lockout. Two weeks later, Picado capitulated and signed an agreement to tighten the reigns on security forces and to established an Electoral Tribunal, which included members of the Opposition, that would be in complete charge of the electoral process (Bell, 1971).

The Election Campaign of 1948 was explosive and divided the nation. Picado's pledge to harness the militia and police was not kept. Adverse public reaction to the government's intimidation served only to strengthen the Opposition's standing in the polls. By the end of Election Day, both sides were charging electoral fraud. Finally, the Electoral Tribunal split two to one in favor of upholding a victory for Ulate. But the pro-Calderón faction held that a split decision nullified the Tribunal's decision and the Calderón controlled congress subsequently voted 27 to 18 to annul Ulate's election victory. It then laid plans for the new congress (whose majority were Calderón supporters) to make the decisive vote for the presidency.

Members of the Opposition Coalition were bitter and just as determined as the Calderón/Picado side to see their candidate become president. Fear and animosity mounted as both sides committed atrocities. Ulate was arrested and Figueres aired publicly a call for men to join him in overthrowing communists and dictators (Biesanz, 1988). Mediation attempts on the part of the Archbishop failed. Within two weeks Figueres began a "War of National Liberation."

Government forces were small, poorly trained, and meagerly equipped. The communist militia and armed Calderón supporters, both allied with Picado's government forces, were more substantial in number but not under a unified command. Figueres's volunteers, including foreigners from the Caribbean League, while fewer in number, were better trained and had superior weapons—partially supplied by Guatemala. After only one month of civil war, 2,000 were dead. The situation was complicated by a Nicaraguan, pro-Picado/Calderón expeditionary force that entered Costa Rica to the north, and rumors that U.S. troops in Panamá were preparing to intervene from the south. Shortly thereafter, on April 18, 1948, pro-government forces signed a conditional surrender that provided exile for Picado and Calderón in Nicaragua, a general amnesty, indemnity to victims and perpetrators alike, and assurances that social guarantees for workers would not be repealed. (This last provision was exacted by Mora Valerder, leader of the communists, who was persuaded by a verbal promise that would allow the communist labor union to continue functioning as a legal organization.)

Figueres was convinced that the First Republic's old political order was irredeemable and promised, therefore, a revolution that would "transform everything." Since his National Liberation Army (whose slogan was "we will found the Second Republic") had been primarily responsible for preventing Calderón's resumption of the presidency, Figueres was in a powerful position to shape the transfer and design of the new government. Figueres believed that, under Ulate's leadership, little would change. But Figueres had also pledged to honor Ulate's election. In compromise, an 18-month interim government, called La Junta Fundadora de la Segunda República (The Founding Junta of the Second Republic) was formed, with Figueres as its president. The junta was intended to oversee the stabilization of the Nation's precarious security and facilitate the election of a constituent assembly that would prepare a new constitution, after which time Ulate would assume the presidency for a full four-year term.

The short-lived Civil War had been the bloodiest episode in Costa Rican history. In its wake it left a legacy of polarized bitterness that lives on as a potent force in the "Second Republic." Coalitions on both sides that were convinced they were fighting for democracy have taken on new forms. Yet the old loyalties and antagonisms that surrounded 1948, personified in Calderón and Figueres, have been expressed undeniably in the election of their two sons to the presidency in the 1990s, representing the two dominant opposing political parties to the present. Contemporary economic and social tensions related to the government's predominant role in guiding development and maintaining social welfare, likewise point back to the 1940s. Finally, in the geo-political context of Latin America, where democracy has been more the exception than the rule, Costa Rica's 1948 experience with the sudden and costly breakdown of its civil and representative governmental system acts as a very real and present reminder to Costa Ricans of the tenuous nature of stability and peace.

---

1. Another notable example of Costa Rican style compromise, from this same period, was the withdrawal of Alberto Echandi Montero from the 1923 presidential race in order to avoid possible violence. His stepping down is remembered as an act of great patriotism. Echandi's departing remark that "the presidency is not worth a drop of blood of even one Costa Rican," is considered a classic example of the spirit of Costa Rican political compromise (Rinehart, 1984, p. 34)

Chapter 3
The Second Republic
and the Rise and Crisis
of the Welfare State (1948-1982)

Introduction

The events surrounding 1948 mark a major turning point in Costa Rican history. Vast changes in the government's role in the economy were given root and grew; reforms initiated by Calderón were expanded under successive administrations to the point where, 30 years later, state expenditures were absorbing 50 percent of GNP. Yet, other pre-1948 systemic patterns retained significant influence. An example is the previous 50-year reign of the liberals and their personalistic leadership. That kind of single party dominance would be replayed during the next three decades, only this time by the PLN with Figueres (the PLN's founder) as the "patron." Whether Costa Rica's reputation as a bastion of stability and a shining example of development is the result of reforms during the Second Republic, or continuity with its earlier history, is a question begged throughout this period's evolution. More central to this chapter, however, is Costa Rica's response to the crisis of 1948 and the onset of the crisis of the early 1980s. The implications for how Costa Rica dealt with these and subsequent crises is the subject of future chapters and significant in the conclusions drawn in this study.

The Second Republic

As president of the provisional Junta Fundadora de la Segunda República, Figueres—who along with his supporters referred to themselves as the generation of 1948—pressed hard to consolidate the reforms that had been initiated in the early 1940s. Social welfare guarantees were respected, and the delivery of civil services was made more efficient. But the junta also instituted a number of additional reforms. Women were granted full political rights. This was a tangible demonstration of the reestablishment of civil and electoral rights, which simultaneously expanded greatly the voting pool beyond the elite, where Figueres's opposition was strongest. (The thriving labor movement, however, was significantly curtailed by restrictive laws enacted since 1948.) The junta also abolished the army, which it considered politically and professionally unreliable. Security concerns were handed over to a reorganized police and a newly established Guardia Civil (Civil Guard). These were placed under the authority of the Ministry of Public Security. (Top positions in both organizations were given to officers from Figueres's National Liberation Army.) Costa Rica realized additional security via its ratification of the Inter-American Treaty of Reciprocal Assistance. Known as the Rio Treaty, the mutual defense pact included the USA as a guarantor against potential aggressors (Rinehart, 1984).

Another important initiative of the junta was the creation of autónomos (autonomous public corporations and institution). These institutions, while public, were intended to resolve economic, social, and technical problems by granting them relative independence from both the legislative and executive branches of the governments. Initially these included the administration of railroads, utilities, public works, public housing, land management, the social security system, health facilities, higher education, and vocational training. But the autónomo that perhaps most alienated conservative and elite elements of the opposition was the nationalizing of the banking system and placing investment and credit under public control. This last measure allowed governmental scrutiny of accounts, which facilitated enforcing the collection of a 10 percent "wealth tax" on bank deposits larger than ¢50,000 (US$10,000). Opposition to these last two reforms, as well as Figueres's leadership, was so heated that a member of the actual junta (its minister of public security) staged a coup attempt. Several lives were lost in putting down the revolt, which exposed the extent of the serious difference that existed even among those in power (Rinehart, 1984).

Internal disgruntlement was exacerbated by the external threat posed by hundreds of Calderón supporters who had fled across the border to Nicaragua. Adding to the pressure, Nicaragua's president, Anastasio Somoza García, was avidly anti-Figueres. When a counter-revolutionary plot against the junta was discovered, Figueres acted quickly in unilaterally abrogating the peace pact made only months before. Members of opposition parties and others who spoke out against the new regime were tried by a makeshift court that granted no appeals of its decisions. Property was confiscated, and opponents within both the private and public sector lost their jobs. The communists, in particular, were singled out for sanctions; several hundred were arrested, communist party unions were disbanded, and its political organ—el Partido Vanguardia Popular (Popular Vanguard Party)—was outlawed. Security concerns on the part of the junta seemed well founded, however. Shortly after these measures were taken, a group of well-armed pro-Calderón mercenaries entered Costa Rica from Nicaragua. Though the population failed to rally behind the insurgents as Calderón had planned, the threat kept tensions high.[1]

Though largely successful at pushing through reforms—834 decree laws in 18 months—Figueres and the PSD failed to see their version of an entirely new "Second Republic" constitution adopted. Instead, the majority conservative constituent assembly (33 PUN representatives and only four from the PSD) merely modified the existing 1871 constitution. The constitution of 1949 did, however, reflect many of the decade's changes. Calderón's earlier reforms, for example, "no longer seemed radical when compared with Figueres's proposals for sweeping change. They soon came to be regarded as part of Costa Rica's heritage, just as happened with many New Deal measures in the United States" (Biesanz, 1988, p. 28). The constitutional congress upheld the abolition of the army, prohibited non-democratic political parties with international ties (in effect the Partido Vanguardia Popular), replaced the spoils system with a civil service, relegated numerous basic services to the autónomos, and extended voting rights to women, blacks, youths, and illiterates (and citizenship to anyone born in Costa Rica), but stipulated that presidents could not run for reelection until at least two other four-year terms had been served by different presidents. Furthermore, unlike most of Latin America, executive powers were curtailed and legislative authority expanded. The new constitution also established what is often referred to as the "fourth branch" of the government, the Tribunal Supremo de Elecciones (Supreme Electoral Tribunal). Appointed to staggered six-year terms by the legislature, members of the tribunal were charged with oversight of the electoral process and were granted police powers, and their decisions were to be definitive and final.

As planned, Figueres and the other members of the junta stepped down after a year and a half, albeit somewhat frustrated by waning support and not having realized the totality of the revolutionary program. The interim government had, nevertheless, set the country on a new course. It had overseen the restoration—or establishment as some would argue—of fair and honest elections and the peaceful transfer of power via political parties rather than a system of personal patronage. (No administration since has come to power by force.) The junta had also moved the political balance further to the left; public participation in the economy and the state's welfare role was henceforth widely accepted. During the next 30 years, political lines would be drawn between left-of-center social democrats committed to the welfare state and center-to-right coalition parties whose platforms championed private enterprise and limited government growth.

Otilio Ulate, the victor from the dubious 1948 elections, served as president of Costa Rica from 1949 to 1953. His administration maintained the programs implemented by the provisional junta, but the 10 percent tax on wealth went largely uninforced and private banks were allowed to compete with the new national banks. Ulate was successful in reducing the substantial external debt he had inherited from the junta. Renewed east-coast banana production and the rising price of coffee on world markets gave a tremendous boost to his efforts. United States aid and a World Bank loan contributed further to the nation's infrastructure and ongoing industrialization efforts.

The relationship between Ulate and Figueres, which had been strained by previous differences, finally broke in 1951 when Figueres formed the Partido Liberación Nacional—PLN (National Liberation Party) and declared himself a presidential candidate in the 1953 election. The broadly-based PLN absorbed the PSD and attracted additional support from liberal and progressive groups with middle class business interests. The party was clearly identified with Figueres and his anti-Calderón/Communist position, but retained affiliate status in the Socialist International and membership in the League of Social Democratic Parties of Latin America. (Figueres was particularly influenced by Peruvian Victor Raúl Haya de la Torre's APRA movement and Jorge Jiménez Volio, who headed the reformist movement in Costa Ricas decades earlier.) As such, the party's platform vested in the state the primary responsibility for promoting societal welfare via a mixed economy that would stimulate growth and distribute income and services fairly and effectively.

Figueres made public his desire to see broader and more open participation in the democratic process and his opposition to personalism. Defusing the decision-making process and organizing the PLN "as a permanent party with ideological substance whose future would not be tied to the fortunes of a single personality or clique" (Rinehart, 1984, p. 54), lent substance to his words. Nonetheless, opponents on either side of the political spectrum considered Figueres an opportunist, charging that the rhetoric of social democracy merely served to advance his own personal ambitions. Indeed, Figueres remained the PLN's leading figure until his death in 1989, and the party retained many of the characteristics of a personalist organization (Rinehart, 1984). He was elected president three times during this period.

The united efforts of the PUN and the PD were insufficient to defeat Figueres who took the presidency in 1953 with nearly 65 percent of the votes. His party also won a majority of the seats in the Legislative Assembly. Figueres's victory represented a clear change in the configuration of the political elite in Costa Rica. It had now broadened to include sectors of the urban and rural middle classes (Booth, 1989). In effect, the Figueres win signaled what was to became a definite shift in power from the long-dominant coffee growers and merchants to university-trained political bureaucrats who were committed to broader interests (Stone, 1975). His party, the PLN, came to dominate politically, "placing itself at the front of a vast capitalist modernization project based on the moderating intervention of the welfare state" (Vega Carballo, 1990, p. 208), and became largely responsible for the direction that Costa Rican society took over the next 30 years. The PLN offered innovation and change while opposition groups offered little in terms of program and had little in common except for their desire to defeat the PLN. The opposition's 1953 candidate, Castro Cervantes, for example, called for a return to order and pledged to free Costa Ricans of the PLN's dangerous experiments and deceitful illusions.

This kind of rhetoric would be repeated countless times over the next three decades and foreshadowed what has today become a fairly predictable pattern of voter response that is consistent with the action/reaction behavior of Costa Rica's political operatives. The election results from 1948 to 2002 were such that the presidency alternated every four years between the PLN and a variety of opposition   coalitions on all but two occasions. (The PLN won back-to-back elections in 1970 and '74, and 1982 and '86.) And until the election of Luis A. Monge (PLN) in 1982, the PLN's platform and behavior in office was largely consistent with its 1951 charter and the idea of Figueres, its founder. (This 50-year PLN dominance was finally broken with the 2002 back-to-back election Victory of the "Unity," a non-PLN presidential candidate and Costa Rica's current president, Abel Pacheco.) PLN administrations greatly expanded public sector employment (from 6.1 percent in 1950 to nearly 25 percent by 1982) and increased benefits, even as government expenditures in health, education, housing and urban development projects multiplied. The number of autonomous agencies grew from 12 when first instituted to an incredible 200 by the early 1980s, absorbing nearly half the national budget. The government and the autonomous institutions had ventured into almost every sphere of influence imaginable.

Many of these developments corresponded with the pledges of PLN politicians. But stated commitments to promote social justice, improve the standard of living of all classes, and eliminate poverty all exacted an increasingly heavy burden on Costa Rica's traditional revenue-producing agro-industries of coffee and bananas, industries noted for their instability. Furthermore, PLN efforts to reduce external dependence by supporting diversified internal manufacturing often meant significant capital expenditures for specialized foreign equipment and went hand-in-hand with hefty import tariffs designed to protect fledgling national industries. Policies during the 1960s and early 1970s actually encouraged industry, to the neglect of agriculture (the country's largest source of employment). Agriculture generated 45 percent of Costa Rica's GNP in 1950 but only 20 percent in 1978. Industry during the same period grew from 12 percent to 24 percent. An important exception to the government's tendency to promote industry over agriculture, in attempts to remedy Costa Rica's heavy dependency on two export crops, was beef cattle. Unfortunately, profits from cattle also proved highly susceptible to the price fluctuations of foreign markets and inefficient use of Costa Rica's work force and land. (Land utilizing a hundred laborers in cultivated crops requires only four on the same amount of cattle pasture.) Diversification via cattle has also been shown to be highly destructive to Costa Rica's delicate environmental balance, with soil erosion, depleted water supplies, and increased natural disasters among the negative consequences (Biesanz, 1988).

The PLN's steady expansion of the state's role in the economy proved extremely expensive (as much as 50 percent of the country's GNP by some estimates, as noted above). With it came national indebtedness, inflation, and economic instability. The party's uncompromising legislative program exacted substantial political costs, too. Detractors abounded. They argued that Figueres's PLN mistook the public sector's rapid growth for genuine economic growth, and that high tariffs and credit redirected from private to public utilization were examples of policies that undermined prosperity. Expropriation and redistribution of unused portions of private estates and multinational plantations by PLN administrations in 1963 and again in 1975 infuriated those affected and mobilized others, who feared they might be next, against the PLN. Conservatives accused the PLN of statism, socialist collectivism, and even communism. These were fighting words for many pro-U.S.A. Costa Ricans during the cold war. The Alianza Socialista Popular (Popular Socialist Alliance) endorsement of the PLN's 1966 presidential candidate actually cost the PLN votes. (Eight years later the communist party regained constitutional legitimacy in a reform backed by Figueres, as a demonstration of the PLN's strength and maturity.)

Opposition campaigns also benefited from the "national desire to avoid concentration of political power" (Vega Carballo, 1990, p. 209). Party strategists preyed on popular fears that two PLN presidents in a row would lead to one-party domination (Rinehart, 1984). Finally, bitter disputes within the PLN itself over government policy and management led to several splits from the party that hurt the PLN in subsequent elections. Although eventually subdued, such infighting contributed significantly to slim coalition victories in the presidential elections of 1958 and 1978.[2] Regardless, the willingness of the PLN early on (1949-1958) to relinquish power to its opposition contributed to the consolidation of the new democratic regime, wherein opposing political forces agreed to accommodate each other and to abide by democratic rules (Peeler, 1985). Although the losing parties in the 1948 Civil War would gradually integrate into political life and adjust to the conditions and limitations of the dominant party, the PLN and its conservative rivals clearly "established an effective working arrangement among major middle-sector political actors and representatives of the national coffee/commercial/industrial bourgeoisie that constitutes the essence of the contemporary Costa Rican polity" (Booth, 1989, p. 395). (This, arguably, has been the case until the 2002 presidential election that was eventually decided in a run-off that gave rise to a new, third party option.)

Despite three coalition presidential victories (in 1958, 1966 and 1978), the opposition was unable to wrest control of the Legislative Assembly from the PLN. (Unidad [Unity Coalition Party] won more seats than the PLN for the first time in 1978 but did not have a clear majority until 1990.) Platforms that promised to improve the position of the private sector, calling for a return to free enterprise and denouncing deficit financing of big government, buckled under the strength of entrenched pro-PLN bureaucracies. Attempts at fiscal reorganization by two coalition presidents, Echandi (1958-62) and Trejos (1966-70), were used against them during the next election campaign by PLN leaders who claimed the coalition's policies had caused stagnation. (Trejos introduced the country's first, and controversial, sales tax.) Rebuttal was usually weak and inconsistent largely because the electoral coalitions of anti-PLN parties had competing policy goals, interests, and personalities. Opposition efforts were often characterized by dissension and lack of direction once in power. Regular failure to limit expensive public work programs or reverse the role of the public sector in the economy led to charges of economic ineptitude from supporters and undermined hopes of developing a sustainable united front against the PLN. The PLN had, in effect, "imprinted its vision of a new social and economic order even when out of power" (Booth, 1989, p.395).

Assertions by opposition groups that the social democratic state's interventionary policies had stifled growth were hard to substantiate. From 1950 to the end of the 1970s Costa Rica's GDP had actually grown at an average annual rate of over six percent. This was the third highest in Latin America. Per capita GDP almost doubled during the same 30-year period, which was significantly higher than any of its Central American neighbors. Other measures of societal welfare similarly improved. By 1980, Costa Rica had by far the highest life expectancy, caloric consumption, and literacy rates in Central America. It also had the lowest disease and infant mortality rates. Indeed, "a prominent (and for Latin America, quite distinctive) feature of Costa Rica's development from 1948 until 1980 was the steady and broadly felt improvement of popular well-being. Income redistribution and improved delivery of public services to the poor increased popular living standards and decreased inequality in Costa Rica between 1948 and 1980" (Booth, 1989, p. 405).

Economic Crisis

Looking back, it is clear that Costa Rica's most severe economic storm was already gaining gale-like force. Though the crisis was clearly not the sole responsibility of the incumbent party, as the next chapter clarifies, it did affect profoundly both major parties' state welfare project, as it had come to be known over the past three decades. The implications for society at large were, likewise, tremendous. Costa Rican economist Claudio González Vega (1984), in reference to this transitional period from the late 1970s through the early '80s, put it this way: "Although the seeds of the crisis had been sown a long time before, one cannot help but be impressed by the degree of change the country has experienced and the speed with which this change has occurred" (p. 351-352).

By 1978, many of the goals of the Junta Fundadora de la Segunda República of 1948 had been realized, and in significant ways a new political and economic culture had evolved along with them. After 30 years at the helm, the leaders of the Second Republic were proud of Costa Rica's progress, achieving growth with equity. Confidence in the premise that "unfettered capitalism causes undesirable and destabilizing socioeconomic dislocations and inequalities" (Booth, 1989, p. 404) shaped the country's economic and political development throughout the period. The state's role expanded steadily, constraining the free market via social guarantees, regulating business, and creating multiple public-sector monopolies, while endeavoring to redistribute revenues among the middle and lower sectors of society. Gary Fields (1986), of the U.S. Agency for International Development's (AID), stated that "no other Latin American country registered so large a decrease in inequality nor so low a level of inequality as Costa Rica" (p. 9.17). According to Joan Nelson (1989), "in 1978, the mood was buoyant" (p.144). National income was lifted to a record level, capping more than fifteen years of brisk growth. This, combined with Costa Rica's good agricultural resource base, its homogenous and largely well-educated middle class (where the political stability of a long-standing democratic tradition was considered the norm), created widespread positive attitudes about the past and high expectation and assumptions about the future. Between 1975 and 1977 real aggregate demand expanded 26 percent. "What was clearly an exceptional episode, in terms of the rate of improvement in real income, was rapidly accepted as the new norm" (González-Vega, 1984, p. 364). By many measures, Costa Rica had become a positive example of the possible in the third world.

Yet even as president-elect Rodrigo Carazo was delivering his 1978 inaugural address, stating that Costa Rica is "an oasis of peace in the world," serious structural problems were already undermining its future. Political economist Eduardo Doryan Garrón, vice minister during the Arias Sánchez administration, reflects back on 1978 as a critical juncture where, in light of past success and recent events, important changes needed to begin to take place within Costa Rica's political economy if a terrible crisis were to be avoided. Doryan laments, however, that neither the opportunities for change nor the danger of impending crisis were part of the political discussions of the electoral campaigns of 1978 (Doryan, 1990). The country could not have been less prepared for the austerity which lay immediately ahead. In reference to 1978, an AID evaluation study of Costa Rica published in March 1983 stated that "no one would have predicted the present outcome even as recently as five years ago" (p. vi). Indeed, from 1978 to 1980 several negative external factors, exacerbated by regional conflict, coalesced with Costa Rica's structural realities to precipitate a severe crisis. Ironically, after two successive PLN administrations—the only time that had happened since the founding of the Second Republic—opposition coalition parties realized their greatest victory over the PLN in the election of 1978, only to soon find themselves in the midst of most severe economic crisis of the Second Republic, accompanied by serious political fallout.

By 1981 Costa Rica's long-term positive economic trends had given way to negative growth: 4.6 percent in 1981 and 6.9 percent in 1982. Unemployment doubled, inflation climbed to over 80 percent in 1982, while per-capita income fell 15 percent and purchasing power by 42 percent. Compounding the crisis, the value of the previously stable Costa Rican currency (the colon) fell, from 8 to 50 to the dollar. Unruly public demonstrations called for the president's resignation while his chief political opponent "predicted that democracy would be 'swept away in a whirlwind of violence' if conditions continued" (Rinehart, 1984, p. 69).

As in other parts of Latin America that suffered severe debt crises during this period—now often referred to as the "lost decade"—Costa Rica lacked timely or adequate data on the extent of its crisis. Since policy makers and analysts both inside and outside of Costa Rica had failed to anticipate the seriousness of the rapid pace of the unfolding events, most analyses and related policies lagged behind reality. This, predictably, made matters worse. Loaded with hindsight, the following pages trace the evolution of Costa Rica's early 1980s crisis and examine its administrations' attempts to cope with public/private forces that continue to have tremendous implications for Costa Rica to the present.

Typically, ineptitude on the part of the Carazo administration from 1978 to 1982, the undependability of Unidad's coalition partner parties, and worldwide recession are cited as the central causes of this crisis. The other most-common finger of blame is pointed at the basic development strategy that Costa Rica had adopted at mid-century (and refined from 1959)—Import Substitution Industrialization (ISI)—which led to excessive public sector spending and state intervention in at least certain sectors of the economy. In sum, Costa Rica's ills that took on crisis proportions at the beginning of the 1980s were the consequence of long-term structural trends in combination with short-term internal and external circumstances. These trends and circumstances were both economic and political in nature.

Structural Trends and ISI Adoption

The effects of Costa Rica's development strategy accumulated steadily after the Second World War, an examination of which lends explanation about the type, depth, and breadth of its crisis. According to González-Vega (1984), several features of the ISI model contradict basic realities within Costa Rica itself. He holds that these contradictions reflect a neglect of crucial economic variables. The consequence of neglecting formidable economic characteristics for thirty years (1950-1980) is that they became incorporated into the country's productive structure (González-Vega). First, Costa Rica's economy has always been very small and limited by a poor domestic market. By the beginning of the 1980s Costa Rica was populated by fewer than 2½ million people. The country's GDP was only about $2½ billion. Considering the small domestic market and the limited and specialized resource base, Costa Ricans typically looked to foreign trade as the key to economic growth. Indeed, as pointed out in the previous chapter, the export of agricultural commodities—especially coffee and bananas—was the most significant contributor to Costa Rica's economic well-being. Levels of domestic output and income rose as did the nation's import capacity—examples of the benefits of export specialization.

A second characteristic of Costa Rica was its high degree of openness to foreign trade; one of the most open economies in the world, according to González-Vega (1984). During the Second Republic exports grew steadily and represented up to 40 percent of GDP (Céspedes, 1983). Imports also increased during the same period, accounting for 25 to 50 percent of GDP. Nearly 70 percent of Costa Rica's agricultural production was exported and earned a similar percentage of the country's foreign exchange. Openness also influenced the expansion of manufacturing in Costa Rica. Between the early 1960s to the crisis of 1980 the export of manufactured goods grew from 4 to 30 percent, although the majority were sold in the protected Central American markets as part of the regional integration efforts of the Central American Common Market (CACM.).

Costa Rica actually adopted an ISI strategy in an effort to lessen dependence on extra-regional international markets and thereby avoid the fluctuations and uncertainties that had come to be associated with economies whose major earnings were tied to the exportation of primary products. ISI theory postulated that the foreign market dependence of small vulnerable economies, like Costa Rica's, would be most effectively reduced by encouraging industrialization for domestic production and consumption. Also know as "desarrollo hacia adentro" (internally-oriented development), influential leaders throughout Central America argued that regional markets offered potential for greater growth and returns and were less volatile than the larger international markets. The 1958 decline in coffee prices that reduced Costa Rica's ability to purchase imported manufactured goods was a principal factor in moving the country's leaders to encourage domestic modern manufacturing industries. Another factor included offsetting the rise in unemployment that had accompanied the coffee crisis and coincided with rapid population growth; local manufacturing would provide jobs for the growing population that, it was expected, would consume more in an expanding home market. Finally as other members of the Central American Common Market began to industrialize (in the late 1950s), and regional economic integration was deepening, Costa Rica was concerned it would be disadvantaged if it did not follow suit (Hall, 1985). Nevertheless, economists like the University of Costa Rica's Juan Diego Trejos (1985) from the Institute of Economic Research debunked the model, arguing that dependency-related problems in Costa Rica actually worsened under its implementation. Diego Trejos, like González-Vega, points out that new industries often required large quantities of imported raw materials and machinery which in turn only further exaggerated trade imbalances and, therefore, dependence.

Consensus in Costa Rica regarding its participation in CACM was lacking, and political turmoil from the mid-1970s-on affirmed the skeptics' concerns about the stability of regional markets.[3] Tying its ISI strategy so tightly to CACM markets was costly for Costa Rica in other ways as well. The success or failure of industrialization has much to do with the size of one's market. Market size "determines the scope for the exploitation of economies of scale and the extent of competition, as well as the degree of viable specialization. Market size also influences the extent to which inward-oriented industrial development may proceed without incurring excessive costs" (González-Vega, 1984, p. 354). The CACM comprised a very small market, and regional integration under CACM resulted in numerous high-cost industries within Costa Rica. These industries were unable to compete once it became necessary to expand into markets outside of Central America. Furthermore, while most Costa Ricans were content with aggregate rates of growth during this period, González-Vega points to a gradual stagnation that reflected the penalization of agriculture and exports that resulted from ISI policies. Average annual rates of GDP growth were seven percent between 1965-70, six percent from 1970-75, and five percent from 1975-80. This decline in growth rates was shared by all major sectors of the economy, but it was actually more obvious in the agricultural sector where rates declined from eight percent to two percent from 1965 to 1980. Early solid rates of growth within the manufacturing sector were the result of an initial spurt in trade among Central American partners that coincided with the signing of the Central American customs union in the first part of the 1960s. Domestic production outpaced domestic consumption when ISI policy was first implemented. Consumption rose and new internally-manufactured goods replaced previous imports that had been the primary source of supply of these goods. But when this early stage of ISI stabilized, the growth rate of manufacturing output decelerated to the level of the growth rate of domestic consumption which was still determined primarily by the nation's exports. González-Vega posits that, had it not been for the externally produced coffee boom of the mid-1970s, the long-term trend toward stagnation and the negative impact on growth of the ISI strategy would have became evident earlier.

Even as Costa Rica's economy was stagnating, ISI protectionist policies were undermining its ability to adjust to external shocks. Developing manufacturing industries to serve the small CACM market required high protection. After taking into account the multiple determinants of protection (duties, tax concessions, investment incentives, credit, and foreign exchange policies), "Costa Rica [became] the most highly-protected country in the region" (Rapoport, 1978, p. 143). Costa Rica's economy became increasingly rigid as protectionist measures implied very high import intensity within the manufacturing sector. This meant that for every 1000 colones worth of output, manufacturers required 800 colones of imported inputs. Costa Rica's dependence on imported raw materials and capital goods deepened as its options narrowed. Throughout this period only 20 percent of imports represented consumer goods. In the event of a negative external shock, balance-of-payment adjustments would necessitate a reduction of imported inputs that would mean a fall in industrial output, investment, and growth, and would eventually affect employment.

While protectionist policies came to distort relative commodity prices as they turned domestic terms-of-trade against agriculture, related policies led to overpricing labor and underpricing capital. Government surcharges tied to labor soon amounted to more than a quarter of all wages. The cost of labor was substantially higher than the salaries received by employees. Though social security, minimum wage, and other payroll taxes were used to finance important public services, wages, especially within the developing manufacturing sector, became greater than the social opportunity cost of the work force. The policies that underpriced capital within this same sector were, as González-Vega (1984) expressed, "the tax treatment of investments, which granted tax breaks on physical capital formation but not on human capital or technological development; the fixed, overvalued foreign exchange rate, which set the cost of imported capital below its social opportunity cost; tariff exemption for capital imports, which increased the rate of effective protection of capital-intensive activities; and the credit-rationing policies that resulted from under-equilibrium interest rates in formal financial markets, which have favored relatively capital-intensive activities" (p. 358).

With factor-price policies and trade policies favoring capital-intensive modernization, labor absorption into what existed of the private sector was minimal. Manufacturing's contribution to GDP contrasted significantly with the proportion of the labor force that it employed; between 1963 and 1973, manufacturing GDP rose 5.4 points while its employees grew by only 1.2 points. In order to counter-balance this trend, government agencies stepped up employment. Since industry's labor capacity was limited, large government bureaucracies evolved to plan, and administer, equity-oriented services – yet another element of Costa Rica's development strategy. During the first 30 years of the Second Republic, public sector employment expanded 7.4 percent, whereas private sector employment grew annually by only 2.7 percent. By the later half of the 1970s, nearly 25 percent of the work force was employed within the public sector. Though Costa Rica had developed an outstanding physical infrastructure, measures of social indicators revealed an equity-oriented system that was very expensive. Along with the rising costs of labor, larger and larger portions of government revenues were consigned to public-sector wages. Predictably as funds for related public goods and services were diverted to wages, the benefits the population had come to expect began to diminish. The government was forced to borrow heavily, domestically and abroad, in efforts to keep pace with the rapid increase in costs of social programs that exceeded income.

These obligations contributed significantly to extensive deficit spending by the government and were a central component in the 1980 crisis. A related trend that accentuated adjustments to the eventual crisis were public-sector unions. Large public institutions facilitated union organization. Over time these unions became the strongest in the nation. They successfully negotiated salaries superior to those for similar work within the private sector and prevailed against any movement to reduce their numbers. Early promises by Costa Rican leaders to meet the welfare needs of the nation that engendered an interventionist state eventually gave way to actual government ownership of many basic industries, known as an entrepreneurial state.

Key to a fuller comprehension of Costa Rica's predicament and its most serious eventual privatizations necessitates the inclusion of prior crucial events surrounding the 1974-78 Oduber administration. Of particular importance is the creation, role and dismantling of La Corporación Costarricense de Desarrollo—CONDESA (The Costa Rican Development Corporation), and constitutes the case study of chapter 4.

---

1. The OAS denounced Nicaragua's support of the insurgents but also cited Costa Rica for facilitating the training of anti-Somoza exiles on its territory. A similar, but much larger, invasion of Costa Rica by Calderón from Nicaragua was repelled in 1955. This followed the implication of Figueres's involvement in an assassination attempt on Nicaragua's President, Somoza García.

2. Figueres, who was reelected president in 1970, was responsible for a pre-1978 party splinter when he made a failed attempt to push through a constitutional amendment that would have allowed him to run again for president in 1978.

3. The subject of regional integration has remained a hotly-contested topic into this century.

Chapter 4
Case Study of Costa Rican Privatization: CODESA

Introduction

Worldwide depression in the 1930s had an important influence on the way the Costa Rican state apparatus was viewed and significantly altered its orientation and organization from the 1940s. Government structures changed as an economic model that focused on heavy state intervention developed. The social democratic victors from the revolution of 1948 sought to transform Costa Rica's antiquated coffee and banana export economy and undo the stronghold on political power exercised by the entrenched agro-exporters. Along with encouraging investors and companies from abroad, these reformers were intent on modernizing industry and creating conditions ripe for the evolution of middle class professionals and businessmen. The National Liberation Party's (PLN) model for a mixed economy corresponded with a process of steady bureaucratic expansion that accompanied state intervention in multiple sectors of social and economic life.

Luis Garita highlights four specific changes as examples of the emerging welfare State in "El proceso de burocratización del Estado Costarricense" (The process of bureaucratization of the Costa Rican State, 1981), that took place in the 1940s:

1. The University of Costa Rica (UCR) is founded as a state university, in the merging of independent academies. Though the cultural repercussions are significant, its impact on economic development was crucial in that the university begins to supply the state with technically skilled personnel and a group equipped to break down the traditional paternalism of the public sector.

2. Social Guarantees and the Social Security System are constitutionally established, laying down the principles for the state in terms of public health, family

protection, labor-management regulations, and provisions for cooperative production units.

3. Price intervention intended to spur agricultural diversity is institutionalized by the opening of the National Production Council. Low-income housing projects are promoted via a similar public entity.

4. New tribunals and government bodies are established as a result of progressive Labor Code laws that challenge the prevailing spoils system and instituted rational public-sector personnel practices.

Garita's (1981) analysis of qualitative and quantitative changes during this transitional period reveals how dominant PLN administrative structures favored public-sector growth. Furthermore, he argues that early on the tendency has been for Costa Ricans to confuse bureaucratic expansion with genuine solutions to structural problems. Accordingly, palliatives in the form of new government institutions were often offered (and sometimes duplicated) but root causes insufficiently confronted. Garita concludes that subsequent enormous state growth (offering better and more sophisticated services with the consent of successive governments and the popular social sectors) was the logical outcome of following a model that did not center on national industrial growth. Instead the state had to compensate for its deficiencies by absorbing excess labor (as agricultural modernization displaced growing portions of the work force) and gave rise to an expanding bureaucracy that was both self-perpetuating and self-protecting.[1]

State intervention expanded during the 1950s and 1960s via macroeconomic policies, in pursuit of a new kind of development that emphasized credit subsidies from a nationalized banking system. Tax exemptions and protectionism went hand-in-hand with the evolving Central American Common Market and created benefits for both domestic and foreign industrialists. During this period the state actively encouraged economic growth, but its actual direct participation was limited, in what Mylena Vega (1982) terms a "estado-gestor." Here Vega's reference is to state intervention largely limited to regulation and provision of services. In the process, power within the executive branch was dispersed and decentralized, passing some responsibilities to new "autonomous institutions." "Autónomos," as they are referred to in Costa Rica, were intended to achieve social goals in nonpolitical ways by minimizing executive and legislative branch involvement.[2]

In the early 1970s, the state orientation as an estado-gestor became increasingly and more directly involved in the productive cycle and capital reproduction. The systematic acquisition of the means of production is how Vega (1982) defines the period and the initiation of what she understands as state capitalism. As the state's role expanded and changed, the independence of the autonomous institutions was curtailed and the concentration of power within the executive branch began to reappear. The state was no longer simply a stimulator of growth within the national economy (interventionist) and a welfare state, but instead became the principal participant. Enterprises were formally constituted as corporations, providing the same legal status as private businesses. Government ownership of numerous basic industries (banking, transportation, agricultural exports, fertilizers, oil refining and distribution, cement, sugar, etc.) created tremendous leverage for the state to direct finite resources toward public-sector enterprises. These types of state industries were most commonly created by La Corporación Costarricense de Desarrollo Sociedad Anónima, or CODESA (the Costa Rican Development Corporation).[3]

CODESA and President Figueres (1970-74)

While the budget of Costa Rica's central government had grown from 127 million colones in 1950 to nearly five billion colones by 1978 (an increase of 15 times per capita), there had existed throughout most of this period an important understanding between the public and private sectors. Consistent with his own background as a successful agro-industrialist, President Figueres had stipulated that the state was to act as an intermediary and stabilizer in strengthening and supporting business within the structure of a mixed economy wherein the state itself would not exact profits (Figueres, 1956). And though Figueres's policies reflected these sentiments, there developed a generational and ideological rift at the center of the PLN that became especially apparent during Figueres's presidential term. Tensions came from a sector that had risen through the ranks of the state bureaucracy, who were middle class and without the private business pedigree of the so called "Generation of '48." Headed by Daniel Oduber, president of the Legislative Assembly at the time, this group was outspoken about its disappointment with the limited results from industrialization efforts (ISI). An attempt by Oduber in the previous decade to promote and finance state-owned industries that would produce basic goods for the national economy had met with stiff opposition within the PLN that killed the proposal. But in 1972, when the Figueres administration backed the creation of La Corporación Costarricense de Desarrollo, CODESA (The Costa Rican Development Corporation), Oduber and his followers found a new opening through which their ideas could be put into practice.

CODESA was set up as a private organization that would include state participation and was intended to strengthen the state's interventionist role in the modernization and growth of economic activities. Figueres insisted that CODESA not develop businesses of its own. Instead, it was projected that CODESA would assist foreign and national companies in creating new businesses, provide technical support to those businesses, facilitate the loan of state funds to private businessmen, stimulate capital markets, and promote exports and development projects. Accordingly, this proposed strategy was assuming a necessary economic function intended to fortify areas of weakness among Costa Rica's private capitalists in order to facilitate new economic activity that supported and complemented the activities of the private sector. In the words of one of its own brochures, CODESA was conceived as

> a system of operations different from commercial banks, that will lend support to the work of the entrepreneur and which, under certain circumstances, will act as an investor by assuming the risks inherent in the early stages of enterprises development, with the intention of transferring the enterprise to the private sector once those risks have diminished and the enterprise is well rooted in the marketplace (Vega,1982).

This was the perspective of the "businessman-politician" (like Figueres) and the reason that CODESA was initially supported by the country's economic elite, important representatives of which formed part of CODESA's board of directors (Cerdas, 1975).[4]

CODESA was a joint venture by law, established as a "sociedad anónima," (corporation) which as such, was governed by the commercial code that exempted it from the comptroller general's supervision. The state was to own 67 percent of CODESA with 33 percent to be held in the hands of the private sector. The sale of government bonds would generate 67 percent of the 100 million colones of authorized capital (or 67 million colones), with the remaining 33 million colones realized from the sale of public shares. The duration of the state's participation was undefined in the related laws.

CODESA and President Oduber (1974-78)

Between 1972, when CODESA was established, and 1976 when it actually entered into operation, an important redistribution of power within the PLN took place that produced significant changes in how CODESA functioned. Daniel Oduber was elected president of Costa Rica in 1974. He and his new generation of PLN functionaries had not obtained the benefits from the previous changes in economic strategy. Unlike their predecessors, who had been businessmen involved with politics, this new group of leaders were middle-class professionals whose careers were tied to government bureaucracies. As "political businessmen" (as opposed to "businessmen politicians"), they viewed their power and influence as connected to "state business" which, in turn, fed the growth of the size and function of the public sector. This class, or social group, that Cardoso and Faletto refer to as the "State Bourgeoisie," also benefited from facilitating the use of foreign credit to finance state enterprises (Cardoso, 1979).

In what Rodolfo Cerdas (1975) would later refer to as the transition "del estado intervencionista al estado empresario" (from the interventionist state to the enterprise state), Oduber made the consolidation of state enterprises the center piece of his political economy (although in efforts to make Costa Rica self-sufficient in its food needs, easy credit to farmers and subsidies to consumers were also provided). As such, CODESA's efforts concentrated on the largest investments that had been financed by the state, while private sector assistance was severely reduced. From 1974 to 1976, 96 percent of CODESA's resources were used to support its own projects whereas only four percent were relegated to the private sector (Vega Carballo, 1980). Several of CODESA's projects also created direct competition with private industries, both in terms of production and access to credit. Furthermore, since CODESA was legally considered a private corporation, none of its projects received the strict oversight by Costa Rica's General Accounting Office that normally accompanied government activities. By the end of 1976 the fast ascending group of "enterprise politicians," backed by a majority in the Legislative Assembly and bolstered by the increased liquidity of large foreign loans and extraordinary high coffee prices, moved to take total control of CODESA. When strong opposition from the private sector attempted to hinder CODESA's progress, Oduber, by presidential decree, eliminated private participation altogether. This action marked the first significant rupture in the union between the state and the private sector since the PLN had come to power in the 1950s, a union that had been maintained throughout the ISI process.

These actions enabled CODESA to finance and execute numerous very large investments under its direct control. According to Doryan (1990), CODESA became the vehicle by which Oduber's new faction intended to gain a certain autonomy with respect to other established sectors of Costa Rica's political and economic elite and to become an active element among the elite. During 1978, 60 percent of public investments were earmarked for CODESA. This transformed CODESA into the country's number one creditor. As such, CODESA came into direct competition with the private sector for available credit, and it also came to be viewed in one form or another as a competitor for funds that had traditionally been reserved for social welfare programs. As a result, distinct private sector associations joined forces for the first time in the Unión de Cámaras del Sector Privado (Union of Private Sector Groups). Together they not only denounced CODESA's expanding role, but the state as a whole. The rapid development of CODESA also divided the traditionally pro-PLN state economic bureaucracy (especially those within the banking sector), between those sympathetic to the demands of the new state political businessmen and those who identified with the desires of the private economic elite. This aspiring new class of government business elite also lost popular support among union and campesino organizations (where support had been strong) when its leaders began to accumulate capital, and charges of corruption proved difficult to refute given CODESA's independence from normal state financial controls.[5]

Adding to these difficulties was a party crisis brought about when José Figueres formed a splinter group within the PLN. Figueres refused to campaign for the 1978 PLN candidate and eventually withdrew from party activities altogether. The situation degenerated further when disgruntled public employees mounted a national strike (which was eventually declared illegal), a plot to overthrow the government was uncovered, and revolutionary activities in neighboring

Nicaragua threatened to involve Costa Rica. Oduber responded by instituting strict security measures and finished his term in office in an atmosphere of political crisis.

In the end, the hasty four-year attempt to bring about an important transformation in the relationships between the various sectors of the elite and to consolidate a new version of state enterprise failed to sustain Oduber's followers in power. Not only did they suffer the worst electoral defeat in PLN history, they also arguably

> did not increase Costa Rica's autonomy in respect to external capital nor develop an effective political infrastructure for their party. And at least among the social sectors tied to national capital, CODESA was not only viewed as highly inefficient in its business ventures, but also greatly hindered negotiations in purchasing goods and services from multinationals" (Doryan, 1990, p. 54).

So despite the important advances in Costa Rican development evident between 1948 and 1978, the strategy implemented by national leaders during the Oduber administration actually increased Costa Rica's vulnerability and external dependence; a reality all too apparent in the economic crises that followed.

CODESA and President Carazo (1978-82)

Rodrigo Carazo Odio, a businessman formally active in the PLN, joined forces with conservative groups and won the presidency in 1978. The winning coalition, known as Unidad (Unity), also won for the first time more seats in the Legislative Assembly than the PLN. While Carazo's promise to maintain the basic elements of the welfare state (though he pledged to do so more efficiently and honestly) may have been politically prudent, it soon began to unravel economically. As a result, not long after Carazo took office, official attempts to privatize CODESA subsidiaries began to take shape (Valverde, 1993). These efforts were opposed by Carazo's PLN opposition. Led by assembly deputy Marcelo Prieto, the new president's former allies succeeded in passing a bill prohibiting the sale of CODESA enterprises to any representative of foreign capital (Rivera, 1982).

The crisis of the Carazo administration began almost simultaneously with his assumption of the presidency. During his first year, international oil prices soared. This marked the onset of a worldwide recession that coincided with his entire four-year term. Interest rates more than doubled on the multiple international loans that the prior administration had successfully negotiated, via CODESA, for its 45 expansive projects. The private sector had also borrowed heavily abroad, owing to the monopoly that the national banking system had wielded over available domestic credit. During this same period, coffee prices plummeted, banana plantations became embroiled in violent labor disputes, and turmoil in neighboring countries curtailed trade with members of the Central American Common Market, which contributed to their default on payments to

Costa Rica and undermined future trade and investment. (Regional conflicts exacted a tremendous political cost from the Carazo administration as well. These included charges of illegal arms trade, weakness in dealing with related domestic terrorism, and using the foreign conflict to divert attention from pertinent economic issues at home.) Costa Rica's public foreign debt tripled between 1979 and 1982, to a point where its total per capita indebtedness was the highest in the world (Rinehart, 1984). The Carazo administration was soon embroiled in the worst recession in Costa Rican history, exacerbated by capital flight, paralysis in foreign investment, and stiffer terms for new international loans. Service on Costa Rica's 1981-82 debt alone would have required the equivalent of 75 percent of the country's total export income. "Economic crisis put this touted paradise on the international financial map for being the first underdeveloped country to suspend debt payments" (Lara, 1995, p. xv).

Administration strategies for dealing with the crisis were repeatedly undermined by division among member parties within the ruling coalition. Support from Unidad's Legislative Assembly majority was undependable, whereas the PLN's strong legislative minority was consistently hostile. Austerity measures designed to cut escalating cost met with stiff resistance, but so did legislation aimed at increasing revenues through heavier taxes and higher charges for publicly provided goods and services. Carazo's written consent to submit to IMF conditions (limited devaluation, reduction in public spending, suspension of certain price controls, and improvements in the tax collection system) in negotiating a 1981 bail-out loan, led the first vice president to announce his refusal to represent the president at public functions. Additional opposition to the agreement was so great that Carazo backed away from implementing the promised economic adjustments. This resulted in the IMF's indefinite suspension of the loan and its eventual withdrawal from Costa Rica altogether. Predictably, presidential decrees became the common last resort of an administration increasingly viewed as erratic, incoherent and ineffective (Trejos, 1985).

The young coalition political party, Unidad, tried to distance itself from the Carazo administration in its 1982 presidential campaign. (Carazo has the dubious distinction as the least-liked president in Costa Rica's modern history.) In an attempt to reignite old loyalties, the party named as its candidate Rafael Angel Calderón Fournier, the son of the former, pre-Second Republic president, Rafael Angel Calderón Guardia. These efforts proved far from sufficient, however, as the PLN candidate, Luis Alberto Monge, took nearly 60 percent of the vote and gave the party its biggest landslide since Figueres's original PLN victory in 1953.

CODESA and President Monge (1982-86)

Victorious in the midst of crisis, Monge had his work cut out for him. While he had campaigned to stabilize and reactivate the economy, he also proclaimed

"that the problem in Costa Rica was 'above all political' and could not be ana-
lyzed solely 'according to the cold criteria of bankers'" (Rinehart, 1984, p. 69).
Monge's reference to the unavoidable relationship between economic and political factors—so often apparent in Costa Rica's past—would become all the more
obvious and determinant in his and successive administrations as the debate over
private versus public ownership, and market forces versus government intervention, unfolded. Valverde, Trejos, and Mora (1993) provide a concise summary of
Monge's role in the debate.

> . . . the Monge administration was interested in preserving the internal market
> and in the industrial and agricultural production geared to that end. . . . It de-
> cidedly favored opening to transnational capital and production for the interna-
> tional market, along with the restructuring of the State. (45)

President Monge's strategy was to create openings in Costa Rica to international
investment, while protecting the country's internal market. In this he received
support from the International Monetary Fund (IMF), the World Bank (WB) and
the U.S. Agency for International Development (USAID). Accordingly, the
president signed letters of intent with the IMF in 1982 and 1985. With the World
Bank, he also agreed to Costa Rica's first Program of Structural Adjustment
(SAP) (Programa de Ajuste Estructural, or PAE in Spanish) (PAE I) in 1985. In
the meantime, he also signed various accords with USAID (Valverde, 1993).

Central to each of these agreements was the implementation of aggressive
measures towards the privatization of CODESA. Monge's hand was strengthened in doing so by the widely perceived need to stabilize the country's economy
following the previous administration's economic debacle. Stabilization included
reduction of spending in the public sector (Trejos and Valverde, 1995).[6] To de-
fuse any remaining opposition to reform measures, the Monge administration
oversaw the creation of the bipartisan National Commission for the restructuring
of the state holding company, according to Decree 16520-P-Mec, of February
25, 1985. The Commission was to review CODESA's status and functioning,
and to make appropriate recommendations to the Central Government. Additionally, the Commission was authorized to sell CODESA assets, to supervise the
process of transfer, and to have final word on any sales of CODESA subsidiaries.

The Commission first turned its attention to ALUNASA, Costa Rica's alu-
minum manufacturing facility. This evaluation was completed in August 1985.
Similar evaluations of CODESA's seven other major enterprises were concluded
by July of 1987. Following each assessment and review by the controller general, invitations were issued to bidders, offers were published in the national
newspapers, specific purchase proposals were submitted, and final sales negotiated and documented with CODESA.

CODESA and President Arias (1986-90)

With the wheels set in motion during the administration of his predecessor, Oscar Arias oversaw the bulk of CODESA's privatization process. Arias signed two more letters of intent with the International Monetary Fund (1987 and 1989), as well as an agreement about structural adjustment with the World Bank (1989). The letters of intent set goals of increasing the country's economic stability and of reactivating its economy through increasing exports (Trejos and Villalobos, 1992). Additional means for achieving such ends included requiring public enterprises to adjust their prices and add tariffs that would enable them to cover costs. Belt-tightening measures included as well the freezing of salaries and the reduction or elimination of regulations on imports and exports. Most important in terms of this study, however, was the requirement to "rationalize" Costa Rica's public sector. This meant intensified insistence on selling CODESA subsidiaries. The necessity of doing so was emphasized clearly in the Conditionality Covenant of 1987 as articulated by the USAID Mission in San José:

> The Mission expects the dissolution, sale, or transfer of the majority of CODESA companies to be completed before the end of 1987. . . . The Mission's . . . privatization objective will focus on continuing to prevent CODESA from creating, acquiring, operating, or financing commercial activities. [The Central Bank] will establish an overall limit of financing . . . to CODESA. . . . The National Banking System will not authorize credit to the National Production Council when such credit is designed to cover . . . provision of subsidies. . . . The intent of the covenant is to reduce the . . . element of subsidized credit. A limit of Central Bank expansion of credit to the economy [will be established, with] a limit on . . . the non-financial public sector. (Quoted in Conroy et al., 1996, p.72)

The directive tone of the USAID expectations left the Arias administration little room to maneuver independently. Either it performed the required privatizations or it would suffer the consequences. The penalties were the withholding of future aid monies and the blocking of aid money already in the pipeline. Arias knew from experience that USAID meant business. In 1984, for example, after the agency had determined that the Monge administration was maintaining a tax on foreign remittances, U.S. disbursements were suspended until the objectionable taxes were removed (Conroy et al.). (Similar examples may be cited from the previous Carazo administration, and later during the Calderon and Figueres-Olsen presidencies.)

The scope of both CODESA itself and its privatization, largely brought to completion under Arias, is indicated by the following list published in the middle of the Arias presidency:

Status of CODESA Subsidiaries, April 30, 1988

Company	Status	Date[7]
Acuacultura, S.A. (Aquaculture)	Sold	1984 C
Algodones de Costa Rica, S.A. (Cotton, ALCORSA)	Sale of Assets & liquidation	9/88 T
Aluminios Nacionales, S.A. (Aluminum, ALUNSA)	Sold to private sector	9/87 C
Atunes de Costa Rica, S.A. (Tuna Fishing)	Sold to private sector	4/87 C
Cia. Industrial Pesca Escama, S.A. (Fishing)	Dissolved and liquidated	1/88 C
Central Azecarera Tempisque, S.A. (Sugar & Alcohol, CATSA)	Transferred in trust to State Agency; to be sold to co-ops & members	9/88 T
Cementos del Valle, S.A. (Cement, CEMPASA)	Assets being transferred to be dissolved & liquidated	10/88 T
Cementos del Pacifico, S.A. (Cement, CEMPESA)	Transferred in trust to State Agency 40 percent of shares to be sold	12/88 T
Consolidación de Compañías Agrícolas Industriales, S.A. (Agriculture)	Disolved and liquidated	1986 C
Consorcio de Exportaciones de Productos Costarricenses, S.A. (Export)	Disolved and liquidated	2/88 C
Corporación para la Desarrollo Agroindustrial (Agroindustrial)	Assets to be sold	5/88 T
Corporación de Zonas Francas de Exportación (Free Trade Zone Enterprises)	Transferred to State Agency	11/88 T
Distribuidora Costarricense De Cemento, S.A. (Cement)	Dissolved and liquidated	1984 C
Ferrocarriles de Costa Rica (Railways)	Assets transferred in trust to State Agency. Dissolved & liquidated	2/88 C

Fertilizantes de Costa Rica, S.A. (Fertilizers, FERTICA)	To be transferred in trust to State Agency. 40 percent of shares to be sold	6/88 T
Guacamaya, S.A	Being dissolved and liquidated	5/88 T
Guanacal, S.A.	Being dissolved and liquidated	6/88 T
Ingenio Tempisque, S.A. (Sugar)	Being dissolved and liquidated	5/88 T
Inmobiliarias Temporales, S.A.	Being dissolved and liquidated	10/88 T
Oficina de Fletamento Marítimo, S.A. (Ocean Fleet, FLEMAR)	Dissolved and liquidated	7/87 C
SEDEMAT, S.A.	Dissolved and liquidated	1/88 T
Tempisque Ferry Boat, S.A.	Assets to be sold	4/88 T
TRANSMESA (Bus System)	Transferred to Office of Public Works	8/87 C
Transportes Aereos Continentales, S.A (Airline)	Being dissolved and liquidated	6/88 T
Centro Permanente de Ferias Y Convenciones, S.A. (Convention Center)	Being dissolved and liquidated	5/88 T
Industria Petrolera de Atlántico, S.A. (Oil Refining)	Dissolved and liquidated	1/88 C
Asufrera de Guanacaste, S.A.	Dissolved and liquidated	1980
MINASA (Mining)	Transferred to Ministry of Energy and Mines	
CODESA seat on Stock Exchange	Retained in CODESA by law	

Examination of CODESA Privatization

It was argued that the elimination of CODESA in the form it had taken from its inception represented a logical and necessary development in the process of helping Costa Rica integrate itself into the New Global Economy. That the state owned cement, fertilizer, mining, and transportation companies in direct competition with private firms offering similar products and services was deemed neither fair nor efficient. After all, the state has enormous resources behind it that threaten to overwhelm most private competitors, thus creating uneven playing fields. At the same time, as USAID policy makers and representatives of the Breton Woods Institutions have pointed out—and as we have seen throughout this study—public ownership is most often characterized by unwieldy and inefficient bureaucratic administration, by wasteful grants, subsidies, and consequent deficits, by cronyism and special interest groups, as well as by widespread corruption (Conroy et al., 1996).

From this view, privatization of state enterprises like CODESA made perfect sense if, by following the direction of the International Monetary Fund, World Bank, and USAID, state direction of the enterprises in question were truly eliminated. However, according to studies like that of Conroy, Murray, and Rosset, state regency has not been eliminated in the privatization process. On the contrary, control of enterprises by the national State of Costa Rica has instead been largely replaced by a "parallel state" represented by USAID itself. That parallel organism established its own bureaucracies. It extends its own subsidies to favored special interest groups, embodies substantial inefficiencies, and is led to corruption not unlike that denounced in official state bureaucracies.

Parallel State

The phrase "parallel state" refers to the IMF, World Bank, and USAID policies of creating, under their control, private sector institutions in the Third World to replace state agencies weakened or eliminated in the process of market liberalization and privatization (Honey, 1994). As referenced above, according to privatization initiatives, USAID in particular assumed many of the functions of the (weakened) central government, making economic policy and compelling the national state to follow its initiatives. Compliance was promoted by a carrot-and-stick approach earlier described when the Monge administration refused to lift taxes on multinational remittances from Costa Rica. More specifically, USAID direction in Costa Rica was intended to support the many aspects of Structural Adjustment Programs, especially the privatization of state industries there (Conroy et al., 1996).

The difference between state structures and their private parallel counterparts was not only one of agency, but also of clientele served. The state offices under attack by privatizers were the products of Alliance for Progress initiatives begun by President John F. Kennedy in 1961. Inspired by a policy of winning Latin American hearts and minds from sympathy with the 1959 Cuban Revolution, Alliance for Progress programs were intended to modernize Latin American countries by establishing economic and political stability and ensuring growth. Pressures were applied to Latin American elites to redistribute land to poor peasants and to institute other resource reallocation projects. In terms used by USAID, government initiatives worthy of aid were to assist "the poorest of the poor," helping them to "meet their basic needs" by creating social welfare programs, which by definition represented government interference in market dynamics (Conroy et al., 1996, p.68).

The Ronald Reagan administration in 1980 brought with it a 180-degree reorientation of USAID policy. Now instead of targeting "the poorest of the poor," programs were to be directed towards assisting entrepreneurial classes, including private bankers, large land owners, exporters, multinational corporations, and local producers who commonly worked with those foreign investors. Those particularly favored in Costa Rica were non-traditional agricultural producers and exporters. The argument was that programs redirected towards entrepreneurs would eventually and more efficiently benefit entire nations. Wealth would "trickle down." The "rising tide" would lift all boats. Thus was born the neoliberal era, the down-sizing of national governments everywhere, and the rise of the parallel state to guide the neo-liberal process away from government-led social-democratic objectives, towards those dictated by market forces.

Among the parallel organizations instituted in Costa Rica was the Coalition for Development Initiatives (CINDE) and the Private Agricultural and Agroindustrial Council (CAAP). CAAP functioned like an export office. Its operations were similar to the government's Centro de Promoción de las Exportaciones (CENPRO). The commission of CINDE and CAAP was to promote non-traditional agricultural exports—helping their producers in the same ways that the Ministry of Agriculture had in the past assisted peasant farmers in the production of traditional crops. USAID assistance was extended to agriculturalists focusing productive efforts not on traditional products such as coffee and sugar, but on crops like macadamia nuts, sesame seeds, broccoli, and cauliflower (Conroy et al. 1996). Between 1986 and 1990 USAID provided CAAP with $35 million of direct aid that bypassed control by the Costa Rican government. In 1988 alone, the U.S. agency provided CAAP with $10.3 million, while the Costa Rican Ministry of Agriculture operated on a budget of only $7.7 million (Conroy et al.).

Besides CINDE and CAAP, USAID created an agricultural university that replicated in many ways (and completed for international funds) Costa Rica's reputable, but under-funded university system. Thus the Regional Agricultural School for the Humid Tropics (EARTH) not only duplicated Costa Rican national institutions, it also competed with the Central American regional Tropical Center for Agricultural Research and Education (CATIE). Additionally, USAID

paralleled Costa Rica's Ministry of Transport by creating its own Asociación de
Carreteras y Caminos de Costa Rica—ACCCR.

Critique of Parallel State

The concern with these new agencies—paralleling existent government institutions such as Costa Rica's Government Export Office, the Ministry of Agriculture, the Agricultural School of the University of Costa Rica, the Central American Tropical Center for Agricultural Research and Education, and the Ministry
of Transport—was that such parallel agencies were characterized by some of the
same problems that had plagued the institutions they were intended to better. An
additional concern was that in several instances they also used Costa Rican taxpayers' resources to finance the parallel state over which the body politic had
little say or control.[8] John Biehl (1988), the Chilean-born advisor to President
Arias, described these concerns when he argued that

> the existence of a parallel structure of bureaucratic organizations to drive Costa
> Rican development is a fact. U.S. economic aid has been conditioned upon the
> creation of several institutions and upon the modification of the laws of Costa
> Rica, all to facilitate a particular model of development. . . . The bureaucracy
> created by this means is enormous. Many of the people that have been hired by
> these institutions have been recruited from the public sector itself, to do similar
> work, but doubling or tripling their salaries.
>
> It is possible—and I make no judgment here—that these entities are good
> for the country. But I do contend that they are financed with public funds. I
> contend that their creation implies duplication, and that therefore they may be
> wasting national resources. I contend that they are not subject to control by the
> National Assembly, nor by the Executive Branch, nor by the Comptroller of the
> Republic, and that probably is not good. . . .
>
> We must be alert against foreigners and their internal accomplices who
> wish to design Costa Rican development behind the back of its democracy
> (p.16A).

Shortly after making this statement, Biehl was dismissed from the Arias cabinet.
However, his observations about and critique of the new economic model and its
administration by a "parallel state" was largely influential both domestically and
abroad, even among AID officials. Biehl questioned what he termed the arbitrary
choice of one development model over another, foreign interference with Costa
Rica's sovereignty, establishment of unwieldy bureaucracies, reduplication of
services, lack of transparency, procedures that entail waste, misdirection of resources, and unaccountable use of the people's money.

Bureaucracy and Inefficiency

In support of Biehl's critique, Lack, Laurent, Espinoza, Christiansen, and Calvert (1989) offer evidence of bureaucracy and inefficiency within the parallel state. According to the predominant standard arguments in favor of privatization, private enterprise qua private is ipso facto more efficient and less bureaucratic. The study by Lack *et al.* questions such pre-judgment, at least in these specific cases from Costa Rica:

> CAAP has developed a substantial bureaucracy and from interviews with the AID project manager inside CAAP, the team had the impression that there are some project implementation bottlenecks owing to CAAP's lack of initiative and excessive attention to bureaucratic detail. These shortcomings have not been conducive to the establishment of an effective implementation strategy. The team also sensed that CAAP was "doing too little of too much" (p. III-9).

The concern here—large bureaucracy, implementation bottlenecks, lack of initiative and bureaucratic red tape, dearth of effective implementation plans, overextension and underachievement—resemble, the complaints leveled against state run enterprises like those located under the CODESA umbrella.

Subsidies and Deficits

USAID was highly critical of price supports and subsidies for peasant producers of basic grains. Yet, the same institution actually afforded large supports and subsidies for the earlier-cited privatized industries that operated under the parallel to the State's Export Office, the Non-Traditional Agricultural Exporters (NTAE). USAID documents expressed worry that the beneficiaries of such generous backing would likely fold shortly after USAID funding ceased (Conroy *et al.*, 1996). In reviewing similar operations in more than ten countries, Lack (1989) and his co-authors observe:

> most of the above institutions are not self-sustaining. In the team's view . . . it is imperative that they implement revenue-generating operations. . . . This will not only help to reduce make-work bureaucracy, but it will also help to reduce dependence on AID (p. III-12).

A USAID (1995) report concluded:

> Less clear is the issue of sustainability of promoter-type projects—or of any trade and investment project. The concept of sustainability means that projects should, within a reasonable amount of time, become financially self-sufficient, or at least be able to support themselves from a combination of revenue generation and contributions from non-AID government, private, and international sources. . . .
> Evidence clearly indicates that investment promotion activities *cannot* support an investment promotion agency without some form of public or pri-

vate sector grant support. Limited experience also indicates that export-promotion activities are not financially sustainable (p. 18).

Special Interest Favoritism

Suggested in the section above, and as earlier indicated, the chief difference between the Costa Rican national state and the parallel entity that USAID nurtured alongside it was the identity of the groups favored as "special interests." Although free trade advocates had criticized the reformist state of unfairly catering to import-substitution industrialists, producers of traditional export crops, small farmers producing basic foodstuffs, and public sector unions, USAID was biased towards other groups. While at first favoring small producers of non-traditional agricultural exports (NTAE), USAID missions switched to more aggressive support of larger producers. In doing so, it followed the recommendation of its commissioned evaluators:

> Although shifting in approach, AID still exhibits a bias in favor of early involvement of small farmers in . . . NTAE initiatives. The nature of these initiatives and the high risks involved, however, call for larger farmers and agribusiness to lead the way.
> Recommendation: AID should spend more time identifying and working with these larger farmers and agribusinesses in NTAE projects (Lack *et al.,* 1989, p.17-18).

Corruption

A common accusation against state run institutions is that they are typically characterized by corruption. While this is often the case, institutions run by the parallel state have been similarly accused. Herbert Beckington, the USAID Inspector General, admitted as much in a classified memo leaked to the press in 1988:

> . . . in 1982 AID and a small group of influential Costa Ricans had formed the Costa Rican Coalition of Development Initiatives (CINDE) to promote private sector economic development. CINDE allowed at least 23 of its former and current officials to evade Costa Rican taxes by diverting AID funds to companies they own through consulting contracts. CINDE created contracts with these companies for consulting services that were not actually provided (Dyer, p.1, 23).

Following the inspector general's report, the Washington USAID office released other audit memos. There it was revealed that "millions of dollars in foreign aids for Costa Rica were mismanaged and misspent, including providing college scholarships for the children of influential citizens and creating a development agency (CINDE) that largely benefited politicians" (Conroy *et al.,* 1996, p.86). Additional revelations showed that $33.8 million of USAID money "was used to establish CINDE in 1982, without proper approval from the State Department. This organization has done little to promote development, but appears to have been utilized by a few prominent Costa Ricans to advance their own personal and political interests, and as a temporary resting place or springboard for aspiring politicians" (Dyer, 1988, p.3). Referencing COFIDESA (Corporación Financiera del Desarrollo, S.A.), the disclosures continued. COFIDESA had received $10 million from USAID in 1982. The *Tico Times* reported that ". . . at least 8 of the institution's 14 directors have taken personal or corporate loans from the money" (Dyer, 1988, p.3). CINDE representatives testifying before the Costa Rican National Assembly protested that "CINDE was never told that it was being given public funds or that it would have to account to the government for their use" (Carvajal, 1988, p.21). As Conroy and his co-authors (1996) comment:

> The parallel state institutions USAID created were not managed with the minimum degree of transparency that one expects from public institutions, nor did their directors feel that they were accountable to the Costa Rican citizenry or their elected representatives (p. 87).

Conclusion

The objective of this chapter has been to examine the process of privatization in Costa Rica within the context of a particular case example—the first of four in this study. The state's behemoth CODESA, which funded and housed more than 40 enterprises, is commonly represented as a clear example of an economic sector in which conversion from public to private ownership and direction seems appropriate and just. In fact, the literature reveals that most analysts, politicians, and economists concur in this seemingly obvious conclusion.

Nonetheless, this review of CODESA's history, including the rationale for its creation and expansion, provides indication that popular sentiment is not without complication. Historical considerations indicate that CODESA benefited many people of Costa Rica. It did so in terms of employment, low cost products, and services, and as a result, the maintenance of social concord along with economic and political stability in a region characterized by strife and chaos. The rule of social law brought in its wake expectations about what the state should do for its citizens. Those expectations have proven difficult to erase. As will be seen presently, especially in the case of ICE (the Costa Rican Electricity Institute) and the CCSS (Caja Costarricense del Seguro Social), failure to meet historic expectations still threatens to tear apart the Costa Rican social fabric.

The passage from state to private ownership, funding, and administration has not been as clean and uncomplicated as is often assumed. The emergence of a "parallel state" greatly influenced by external actors, often in favor of a local entrepreneurial elite, not only challenges Costa Rican sovereignty and potentially weakens social stability, it has perpetuated some of the very features privatization was intended to eliminate—bureaucracy, inefficiency, cronyism, and corruption. Additionally, the parallel state also turns over to outsiders the administration of taxpayer colones for expenses uncontrolled by their elected representatives.

None of these observations in itself invalidates the rationale behind the privatization of CODESA—which in any case remains a fait accompli. It may simply be that the dysfunctions indicted resulted from the immaturity of the process in question. Conventional wisdom may be correct. Operations like CODESA have seen their day. The post-Cold War world has moved beyond state ownership of cement, fertilizer, highway, mining, fishing, and agricultural operations.

However, CODESA's case *does* raise some concerns that will be tracked through the remainder of this study, namely weighing the social costs and benefits of privatization designs. Do indices of growing unemployment and rising crime outweigh favorable fluctuations in Gross National Product? Do privatization programs significantly reduce bureaucracy and inefficiency? What of the matter of replacing public elected bureaucracies and their inefficiencies and corruptions with private, corrupt, and inefficient bureaucracies over which ordinary citizens have no say? Each of these questions will re-present themselves in the chapters that follow.

---

1. Diego Palma (1980) reaches a similar conclusion in "El Estado *y* la Desmovilización Social en Costa Rica," but for quite different reasons. Palma argues that the Costa Rican state's capacity to absorb social conflict results from the political ability of its dominant-class to channel demands of the poor through new government institutions that partially ameliorate this group's sense of urgent need. This also limits popular participation. In what Palma terms a "hegemonic relationship," dominant-class interests are preserved in a kind of compromise that co-opts and effectively demobilizes opposition among the common citizenry. This is contrasted with the "coercive" means employed by other regional elite in El Salvador, Guatemala, and Nicaragua, wherein violent repression is used to quell protest. While Palma recognizes the benefit within Costa Rica where there are fewer violent oligarchic expressions, he nevertheless views many of the elite's legal, political, and ideological methods as shortsighted, misleading, too costly, and ultimately misguided true democracy (pg 183-206).

2. Compromises were made in the mid-1960s to correct what "autónomos" critics felt had led to institutions that were too large, too prolific, had too little accountability, and lacked intra-governmental coordination. Social Security (CCSS) and Electricity and Telecommunication (ICE) are two "autónomos" that have retained a particularly large degree of autonomy and are often cited as examples of successful "autónomos" (Fernández Pinto, 1976).

3. Though the Costa Rican Petroleum Refinery (RECOPE) was actually nationalized in 1963, only 15 percent was owned by the state. With the establishment of CODESA, however, the state came to control 65 percent by 1973, 80 percent in early 1974, and a

full 100 percent of RECOPE shares by year's end. RECOPE was an important piece of the state capitalist project (and came to finance other related state enterprises) but never provoked the kind of serious conflict among the industrial capitalist sectors as did CODESA. In explanation, Vega (1982) argues that RECOPE nationalization, amid the early 1970s energy crisis, was broadly accepted by major sectors who understood that the state was an appropriate agent to take charge of this strategic area within the economy that involved the interests of capital as a whole.

4. The Costa Rican Chamber of Industries believed CODESA provided a necessary complement to the process of domestic accumulation of capital. These industrial sectors felt the process had been inadequate due to weak capitalist development. In subsequent years, the Chamber questioned and withdrew the support it had initially given.

5. Incorporated as "sociedad anónima," CODESA enterprises and subsidiaries did not have to submit to public bidding when it came to the purchase of materials or equipment, which certainly facilitated those bent on unethical gain.

6. The bitter pills of layoffs and other belt-tightening measures associated with these reductions were eased by sharp increases in U.S. aid to Costa Rica during the 1980s. The aid was considered necessary as the United States advanced its policy of counter-revolution throughout Central America, especially in Nicaragua. Costa Rica was the only stable country in the region, and the purpose of U.S. assistance was to keep it that way—as an example of a successful capitalist economy in a region influenced strongly by socialist tendencies. To make it such, the country became the recipient of monetary aid reaching levels of $1,000,000 per day. This enabled both Monge and his successor, Oscar Arias, to camouflage economic and administrative deficiencies in ways that were unavailable, for instance, to Carazo.

7. In this column, "C" indicates process completed; "T" indicates target date for completion. Also the process of dissolution and liquidation takes approximately six months, in order to comply with Costa Rican law. In the case of CODESA subsidiaries an additional period of restructuring, accounting, and legal research was required.

8. CINDE and other institutions sponsored by USAID were purported to be 100 percent funded by the agency's budget. However closer examination of the funding process shows how some, like Arias advisor John Biehl, reached the conclusion that Costa Rican taxpayers actually ended up paying the bill. According to Conroy et al. (1996), the process involved five steps: (1) USAID deposited $700 million in the Costa Rican Central Bank, awaiting disbursement to Costa Rican institutions; (2) the Central Bank paid market interest rates on the deposit (averaging 21 percent); (3) over a five-year period, USAID thus collected $100 million in interest; (4) that money—provided by Costa Rican taxpayers—was then used to finance the private sector initiatives USAID wished to sponsor; (5) in the process, the deficit of the Costa Rican Central Bank increased, with 1/3 of the increase traceable to the interest paid to USAID (Conroy et al., 1996, p.81-82; see also Shallat, 1989).

Chapter 5
Case Study of Costa Rican Privatization: ICE (Energy and Telecommunications)

Introduction

This chapter examines various attempts to privatize Costa Rica's national electricity company, the Instituto Costarricense de Electricidad (ICE), which according to Articles 188-190 of the National Constitution is charged with providing electrical and telecommunications services to the country. It represents a public service essentially different from CODESA (see chapter 4) which has numerous privatizations and whose companies offer products in markets where private firms compete in a for-profit environment. The ICE, on the other hand, offers services in what some high-profile political actors have argued is a natural monopoly (Aguilar Sánchez, 2003). They maintain that, especially in a country the size of Costa Rica, it would make little sense for competing companies to install multiple infrastructures to generate and deliver electrical current, or telephone, radio, or television services. Maria Lourdes Echandi Gurdián (1996) explains:

> A natural monopoly occurs if a given level of production, whatever the product might be, can be achieved in the least expensive way by one firm rather than by two or more. When "economy of scale" considerations make that possible, we have a natural monopoly. . . . Markets exist in which competition is not desirable, or not even viable. If the production in question has important economies of scale, such that in the long or medium run costs diminish as production increases, it is more efficient to have a single producer than many firms competing with one another. In those natural monopolies competition is not desirable, because the existence of more than one producer raises costs. . . . In such circumstances the adoption of anti-monopoly measures to impede the establishment of a natural monopoly would be counter-productive (p. 23).

Privatization purports to simplify a company's operational objectives via exposure to the forces of market competition, thereby reducing costs, increasing output, and generally improving performance. Vickers and Yarrow (1988) made a comprehensive study of the contribution of ownership to industry efficiency. Their findings indicate that only in firms where healthy competition existed was private ownership superior to that of public ownership. Where competitive forces were absent in the market, Vickers and Yarrow concluded that introducing competition (i.e. by eliminating monopolies), or regulations that created conditions similar to competitive forces, likely provided for greater gains in efficiency than could be anticipated from the shift of ownership to the private sector. Efficiency would increase minimally by exchanging a private monopoly for a public monopoly, and if so, according to this study, primarily as a result of reduction in the work force and the restriction of services to markets that promised a higher probability of financial return.

Costa Rican telecommunications spokesman Gerardo Fumero (2004) argues that a natural monopoly exists in the telecommunications field, especially in a country the size of Costa Rica. There it would make about as much sense for competing companies to install multiple infrastructures to generate and deliver electrical current, or telephone, radio, or television services, as it would for private companies to build a "competing" highway system for the country (Fumero). Moreover, the introduction of competition into the provision of Costa Rica's electrical and telecommunication services would eventually resolve itself into a private monopoly or oligopoly in any case ("Temor a la competencia?"). This would occur even if ICE itself were not privatized but merely forced to compete with private companies. Those companies, would eventually drive "ICE as we know it" out of business.[1]

Clearly, state-owned ICE operated in a market lacking competition. ICE supporters are convinced that Costa Rican reality implies an economy of scale that makes it impractical to support more that one efficient enterprise.

Even without natural monopoly considerations, the ICE represents a case apart, since it is an intentionally non-profit institution. Its constitutional purpose was to provide electricity and communications services even to those with extremely limited financial resources (Fumero, 2004).

ICE's attempted privatization is a work in progress. The Instituto, unlike CODESA in the previous chapter, has not yet been fully privatized, and the debate concerning that eventuality is not nearly finished. Moreover, the controversy has mobilized the entire country of Costa Rica. The issue's context is one filled with promises made and retracted or broken and with huge demonstrations involving students, labor unions, women's groups, public employees, and environmental activists (Wolkoff, 2000). The debate has centralized charges and counter-charges, payoffs, and corruption scandals. All of these demonstrate many of the issues, and much of the dynamics that often surround privatization debates in general. In sum, the ICE represents an important case study in the examination of an additional dimension of Costa Rica's efforts at privatization.

Given that privatization and economic reform are often used synonymously, even though economic theory suggests some ambiguity in its ability to assure its practitioners that an enterprise's economic efficiency (or the economy as a whole) will necessarily improve under private ownership, it seems useful to examine the initial experiences of Costa Rica's ICE with privatization programs and their contribution to the success of market-based reforms undertaken from the crises of the early 1980s to the present.

With that in mind, this chapter will review ICE's stated purposes and the controversies surrounding the three major ICE privatization proposals. Although some proposals were formulated as early as 1981, the first serious proposition emerged in 1987. A second even more vigorously-contested initiative, the so-called "Combo-Bill" of 2000, will also be examined. Currently, the county is embroiled in debate about a blanket privatization proposal in the form of the Central American Free Trade Agreement (CAFTA). This chapter will address this proposal as well—in connection with an evaluation of the free trade and privatization claims advanced in the CAFTA debate.

Instituto Costarricense de Electricidad (ICE)

The Instituto Costarricense de Electricidad was a product of the Costa Rican "war of 1948" (referred to earlier by some as the Costa Rican Revolution) and the subsequent institution of the Second Republic. ICE's purpose was to create part of the infrastructure considered essential for the nation's industrial development (Salas, 1995). The Institute was founded according to Law No. 449, passed on April 8, 1949. That law described the basic functions of ICE in these words:

1. To provide swift and efficacious solution to the problem of the country's scarcity of electrical power wherever such scarcity exists, to seek the provision of constant useable energy to satisfy normal demand, and to encourage the development of new industries as well as increased domestic use of electricity in rural regions. The principal activities of the Institute will be to fulfill this objective, using all the technical, legal, and financial means necessary, and its basic program will be the construction of new hydro-electrical plants and networks necessary for the distribution of the plants' production. This project will be pursued within limits described by investments that are economically justifiable.

2. To promote industrial development and increased national production made possible by the preferential use of electrical energy as the source of power and heat and, assisted by means of consultation and technological research, to promote the enhanced understanding and exploitation of the country's resources of wealth.

Commenting on the legal formulation, the co-founder and co-developer of ICE, Jorge Manuel Dengo (1997), summarized its five underlying premises:

1. The elaboration of a national policy of strategic energy control as an element fundamental to the development of the country.

2. The creation of an evolving institutional structure in accord with the needs addressed by the institution in question.

3. The formulation of a clear financial plan for the Institute's future.

4. The formulation of a long-term guiding plan, second in importance only to the goals of nationalism.

5. The development of optimal professional and administrative training (p.77).

Important to note in both the law's formulation and in the words of ICE's co-founder is the primacy of place given to nationalism, to energy control as the key element under that heading, and to the (industrial) development of Costa Rica as the implied principal means for achieving specifically Costa Rican national development. In the 1949 context, the extension of electrical services to the farthest corners of the country was central to the national project of industrialization. The extension was to be accomplished with financial efficiency ensured by competent direction of the required structural apparatus.

In 1963, ICE's function was expanded beyond the production of electricity to include telecommunications. On October 28, Law No. 3226 was promulgated empowering the Institute to provide telephone, telegraph, radio, and radiotelegraphic services to Costa Rica both nationally and internationally (ICE, 1988a).

More specifically, ICE was charged with maintaining the electrical and telecommunications networks of the entire country. This included planning, designing, constructing, and activating those networks. Additionally, the Institute was to expand and maintain the required generating plants, substations, transmission lines, and distribution networks of its electrical sector. ICE was responsible for the expansion and maintenance of the centers, networks and other elements necessary for fulfilling its telecommunications responsibilities (ICE, 1988a).

ICE was placed under a Directive Council, also referred to as the Junta Directiva. The council was headed by an executive president, with six directors under the executive's authority. Council members were to be appointees of the Republic's government that would then set policy for the institution.

The Instituto Costarricense de Electricidad was to be financed by revenue generated by the services it provided, by floating bonds, and also by funds received externally, e.g. from loans by international development banks and from "soft loans" granted by industrialized countries for purposes of "foreign aid." Nevertheless, ICE was to remain a non-profit institution, offering all of its services at cost. As a public service entity, the Instituto Costarricense de Electricidad was also commissioned to sponsor cultural programs, including artistic exhibitions and conferences in Costa Rica's main population centers, e.g., San Jose, Alajuela, Heredia and Cartago (ICE, 1988a).

A close affiliate of the ICE is the National Power and Light Company, Inc. (CNFL) founded in 1927 by the American Foreign Power Company, a subsidiary of the U.S. firm, The Electric Bond and Share Company. By 1928 this company held monopoly control over electrical services across the Central Zone of Costa Rica and had absorbed all other providers. From that time on the CNFL was the principal distributor of electricity in the country. Following the formation of ICE, and since 1958, CNFL became the second-ranked provider in terms of its productive capacity. In 1968, by virtue of Law No. 4197 (September 1968), the ICE acquired 93.74 percent of CNFL shares, thus gaining control of the company's policy as well as its board of directors. ICE also controlled the appointment of its director and auditor. Meanwhile the remaining 6.26 percent of shares were held by Costa Rican investors (ICE, 1988a).

Other firms generating electricity for Costa Rica include the Electrical Unions of Alajuela, Heredia, and Cartago, as well as smaller municipal and private companies. The ICE serves Costa Rica's Central Zone and generates approximately 72 percent of that area's electrical energy, thus leaving about 28 percent for the other companies (ICE, 1988b).

The supply of electrical current to ICE's clients is generated principally by Costa Rica's rivers, which energize turbines at hydroelectric plants. The main rivers are Arenal, Corobici, Rio Macho, and Cachí. These rivers produce 97.37 percent of the country's total electrical output, with the remaining 2.63 percent produced thermoelectrically, by wind, and by plants fueled by petroleum derivatives. Each client's consumption is monitored by a meter, which is read each month to determine the corresponding monthly electrical bill (ICE, 1988a).

Privatization Initiatives

Despite ICE's general success in achieving its goals, the global economic crisis that embroiled Costa Rica brought her public institutions into question and gave impetus to proposals for the privatization of the Institute from 1981 onwards (Salas, 1995). As discussed in chapter 3, the economic crisis of and political fallout from the early 1980s was largely quelled by huge inflows of international aid in a effort to assure stability. This point was aptly made as part of an independent investigation of that period: "However much cynicism there is about Costa Rican claims to 'exceptionalism,' the continued preservation of a liberal and free Costa Rica is seen in Washington and in Central America as evidence that non-Communist societies can survive in the region" (Sanders, 1986, p.6). Nevertheless, by 1986 the campaigns for the Costa Rican presidency found the platform of the two leading candidates from opposing major parties strikingly similar in their support of the thesis that the economy needed restructuring; there was fair certainly that the foreign assistance, muffling the crisis, would not last forever.[2]

From then on, over the objections of labor unions, and despite the continued ability of ICE to construct and maintain the necessary infrastructure, engineering contracts began to be outsourced to private companies. These included blueprints for control stations and electromechanical installations. Thus the Department of Public and Electromechanical Works began to be dismantled, along with its Office for the Construction and Maintenance of Plants and Substations. Workers displaced in the process were transferred to other posts within the ICE; others were retrained for new responsibilities (Salas, 1995).

In 1987, the second year of the Arias administration, fourteen activities, argued to be "non-strategic" within the Instituto Costarricense de Electricidad, were transferred to the private sector. After some internal debate questioning their designation as "non-strategic," the areas privatized included (a) janitorial, security and messenger services; (b) tax collection; (c) radio transmission to rural areas and maintenance of public telephones; (d) electrical connections in rural areas; (e) building maintenance; (f) distribution of telephone and electricity receipts; (g) construction of telephone lines and centers; (h) construction and enlargement of one-story civic buildings; (i) building of airport interchanges; (j) maintenance of rural electrical and telephone centers; (k) maintenance of existing mobile phones; (l) design and construction of electrical and telephone lines; (m) data processing and software design; (n) network testing (Salas, 1995). (An argument questioning the constitutionality of theses privatizations is laid out in the following chapter that deals with the Costa Rican Caja.)

An ICE-Initiated Privatization Proposal

Two privatization proposals that surfaced over the last 25 years merit special attention. For ICE, the most important privatization initiative originated within the institution itself. It took the form of a proposal to the Legislative Assembly from the Institute's own administration. Presented as a response to Costa Rican president Oscar Arias's appeal for ideas about the economic democratization of the country, the proposal was bolstered by appeal to financial and technical problems, with special reference to the lingering effects of the energy crisis. According to the ICE's board of directors, the Institute had lost its autonomy; it lacked training in finance, and was faced with major changes in telecommunications technology. ICE administrators were joined in their drive for privatization by powerful members of the majority National Liberation Party (Partido Liberación Nacional [PLN]), even though this position contradicted the longstanding economic stance of the international Social Democratic tradition of which the PLN was a part. This created internal party fissures that continued to widen until 2005, when the PLN experienced serious splits. The country's number one conservative newspaper, *La Nación,* also sided with the ICE administrators as did important sectors of the opposition Social Christian Unity Party (PUSC).

Accordingly, the ICE board of directors proposed "restructuring and modernizing" the Institute, granting it increased autonomy. The board requested a 60 percent raise in electricity rates for 1989, with additional 5 percent and 10 percent raises over the next two years (Salas, 1995). Also recommended were cost-saving measures such as selling in the form of shares 60 percent of the state's telecommunication services and 40 percent of its power and light industry—giving priority in such sales to employees and associates. Additionally, the ICE board suggested seeking subsidies from other unspecified sources (Salas, 1995).

In response to this request, the ICE administration was directed to consolidate the National Power and Light Company (CNFL) and ICE itself to form a single entity. Forty percent of the resulting single enterprise was then to be sold to private investors. Later this directive was limited to the sale of telecommunication shares only (Salas, 1995).

Labor Union Resistance

Strong resistance to the privatization measures just described was generated by the nine labor unions whose workers were employed within ICE. These formed an umbrella organization to resist the efforts to privatize the Instituto Costarricense de Electricidad. The organization was called Labor Union Front (Frente de Organizaciones Laborales [FOL]). While subscribing to the Front's opposition to privatization in general, member organizations differed over the question of how much privatization to allow. That is, the FOL recognized that privatization of state services took different forms. As noted earlier, these ranged from total privatization (i.e. absolute sale of state businesses or industries to the private sector), to the sale of shares in the state enterprises (with the ancillary economic stimulation inherent in such sale), to the outsourcing of consulting and design services, to minor activities, such as the repair of state vehicles. While all group members of the FOL objected to the first and second types of privatization, the engineers' union and the technicians' union differed in assessment of the other forms. More specifically, the engineers' union considered the privatization of secondary services permissible. The technicians union, on the other hand, saw such permission as an "entering wedge" which brought with it the risk of mounting a slippery slope towards less acceptable forms of privatization (Salas, 1995).

Additionally, Costa Rican labor unions assessed ICE privatization efforts as resulting from the state's transfer to the Institute itself of costs unrelated to ICE services. That is, Costa Rica's large external debt necessitated systematic devaluations of its currency, so that foreign exchange debt repayment had to be made with a local currency of constantly diminishing value. This caused the nation's cash-strapped central government to search for revenue sources wherever available. In such circumstances, the Instituto Costarricense de Electricidad presented itself as a cash cow. The privatization of its infrastructure and/or services promised to produce revenues useful for lowering the country's debt obligations, which was a condition tied to continued international loans.

To support such analysis, the FOL called attention to the fact that although Costa Rica's external debt had been restructured in 1990, the ICE was obliged to continue making its contribution to debt repayment as though the debt restructuring had not taken place. Thus in 1991, the Institute was required to increase its rates by 35 percent, while the tariff enhancement should have been only 10 percent, had the country's debt restructuring been taken into account. Such a drastic increase gave the impression of inefficiency on the part of the ICE, thus contributing to the perception that the enterprise (or at least its principal activities) should be privatized. According to the FOL, this was precisely the perception favored by Costa Rica's external loan benefactors—as well as by the country's internal financiers (Salas, 1995).

FOL resistance to privatization was countered by pro-privatization justifications stemming from ICE's alleged lack of autonomy, resulting from oversight by the central government's bureaucracy. This handicap, it was argued, impeded the development of the Institute and thus became an argument for privatization. For instance, private enterprises had more flexibility in downsizing the labor force and therefore could save money in labor costs. Typically, private enterprise was also more technologically advanced and, free from obsolete laws, had the ability to more unrestrictedly adopt technological improvements with less delay. Indeed most policy makers who advocate the replacement of government decision-making with private ownership do so on the grounds of efficiency gains. Governments are understood to often pursue multiple objectives in the management of their institutions. Common among these, and consistent with this Costa Rican case of the ICE, are job creation and the provision of services to population sectors or geographical regions that are not commercially profitable. These "divergent" objectives are in part responsible for what the World Bank has referred to as disincentives that reduce efficiency and, therefore, institutional profitability. Though mostly critical of public-firm performance in the developing world, the World Bank noted that "bureaucrats typically perform poorly in business not because they are incompetent (they are not), but because they face contradictory goals and perverse incentives that can distract and discourage even very able and dedicated public servants" (World Bank, 1995, p.3).

Resolution of the Debate

A turning point in the debate about privatization of the Instituto Costar-ricense de Electricidad came in January 1988, with a court arbitration hearing. In Costa Rica, "where the emphasis is always on political consensus" (Sanders, 1986, p.6) (a dynamic described in chapters 2 and 3), the hearing was petitioned by ICE workers, who received a favorable decision in the middle of the year (Salas, 1995). That decision established a formula for automatic salary increases for union members of professional status, thus depriving the ICE administration of any hope of support from the professionals within the organization relative to the privatization controversy. Additionally, the results of the arbitration created conditions for greater autonomy within ICE itself, as well as for more extensive managerial responsibilities for workers within the Institute. Accordingly:

1. A Labor Relations Board was formed, whose membership consisted of Institute authorities and labor union representatives. The Board would oversee firings and disciplinary measures.

2. Two bi-partisan boards were established to oversee administrative careers and occupational health. The former ensured that all promotions and new hires would emerge from strictly-regulated competitions.

3. Salary increases would be awarded in accordance with market studies, and extended independently by ICE.

4. The Institute would enjoy increased autonomy in administrative matters with greater worker participation in pre-defined situations.

This measure not only gave workers a stronger identification with the ICE, but ensured greater solidarity among them relative to discussions of privatization.

Even before the workers obtained their favorable court decision, the Political Directorate of the National Liberation Party and the party itself adopted an official position against the privatization of ICE although this contradicted the desires of important party members, including the country's president (Salas, 1995). In doing so, both cited the weakness of the proposal brought forward by the Institute's board of directors. Additionally, the government's current and previous minister of planning rejected the proposal on technical grounds. Nevertheless, the ICE administration continued to support privatization, along with *La Nación* and influential neo-liberal economist and politician Thelmo Vargas.

None of this, however, is to say that the Instituto Costarricense de Electricidad somehow escaped the debate unscathed, even from its supporters. Virtually all participants in the discussion acknowledged the presence of serious deficiencies within the Institute. Nearly unanimous as well was the judgment that the ICE could not continue to offer its services (both for electricity and telephone) below true market value and that its service rates should therefore be increased. This judgment placed in full debate the policies of state social enterprises. In fact, the minister of planning declared that electricity should not even be included in the basic-necessities basket (Salas, 1995).

Shortly after the arbitration decision had been reached, its strength was tested. ICE's board of directors sought public licensing for a cellular telephone project involving transnational corporations (TNCs). Union officials denounced the project on the grounds that the TNCs involved had unfairly influenced the negotiations and had improperly channeled biased information to National Assembly members (deputies) who would decide the matter. Deputy Javier Solis characterized the project as a breach of national security, as did the ICE Union of Engineers. An official government investigation ensued. In the course of events, the FOL not only prepared a counter-proposal but also organized meetings, marches, and national round-tables to discuss privatization and the reasons for opposing it. In doing so, it offered technical and statistical arguments for adopting its position. The FOL mounted a lobbying campaign to influence deputies, Institute directors, and political leaders. The whole process resulted in the mobilization of anti-privatization opinion across broad sectors of society.

In this way, any hope of pushing through an ICE privatization plan without discussion was squelched. President Arias authorized a blue ribbon commission to discuss the reorganization of the Institute. The commission included deputies, as well as the country's vice president, delegates from the ICE board of directors, FOL representatives, and the minister of Energy and Mines. Thus the project of ICE's privatization was questioned and de-legitimized (Salas, 1995). It was formally rejected on October 6, 1988.

Nonetheless, the debate about ICE had been irremediably changed as a result of the foregoing sequence of events. The business sector had secured a permanent place at the table. In addition, public consciousness had been raised about low electrical rates in relation to inflation. This enabled the executive to call for a series of reforms that would exercise influence on future discussions about ICE privatization. These included the conservation of electricity and its more efficient use, the promotion of electrical generation in small and medium sized private plants, the raising of ICE electricity rates sufficient to offset future investments, and the granting of increased flexibility and autonomy to ICE.

From this first major confrontation over ICE privatization, it is possible to draw the following conclusions.

1. The administration was prevented from realizing its privatization goals by a series of contextual elements over which it had little control, and according to prominent political scientist Rodolfo Cerdas, "the representatives appear (ed) only to represent the interests of themselves and sectors that do not closely identify with our social reality" (Palmer, 2004, p.347). The community at large identified with the Institute as preventing an important energy resource from falling into foreign hands. This identification extended to the institutional representatives who benefited from personal identification with ICE.

2. The whole privatization debate strengthened workers' organizations connected with the Institute. It helped them succeed in a unification project that successfully incorporated professionals and less-skilled workers. This enabled workers to successfully formulate the medium-term plan that eventually carried the day.

3. Similarly, workers had gained a permanent place at the table where privatization issues were discussed. They had succeeded in connecting considerations of salary and working conditions to privatization policies.

4. Although the privatization of ICE, in terms of selling shares, was successfully blocked, the "rules of the game" had been changed at the Institute. Rate hikes were approved and excluded from the basic services basket.

5. Despite worker input and the contributions of various social sectors, it is evident that there was insufficient political will or agreement to grant ICE the autonomy it needed to make the changes necessary to improve its services as provider of telecommunications.[3]

The ICE Combo Proposal

In April 2000, President Miguel Angel Rodriguez, who headed the conservative Partido Unidad Social Cristiano party, proposed a bill for "modernizing" the Instituto Costarricense de Electricidad y Telecomunicaciones. His proposal for a combined packet of measures, popularly known as the "ICE Combo Bill" (in the parlance of the prolific foreign fast-food industry in Costa Rica), advocated transformation of the ICE into a public business that would compete freely with private-sector firms (Brooks, 1999). That is, rather than outright privatization, the law would permit Costa Rica's government to license private companies to compete directly with the ICE and Radiografica Costaricense (RACSA) in producing and marketing communications and electrical services. Such private provision of services would be permitted starting five years after the law's passage. Meanwhile private Internet services could begin within one year.

Under the new law's provisions, ICE itself would undergo an extensive process of restructuring. It would become a semi-autonomous corporation controlled by a government-appointed board of directors. Thus revamped, the Institute would be subdivided into four companies: an electric company (Compania Nacional de Fuerza y Luz, CNFL); an electric-power generation and distribution company (ICELEC); a data-transmission service company (RACSA); and a telephone company (ICETEL). Under this arrangement, ICE itself would not be privatized. It would remain in control of 51 percent of the private-sector concessions given by ICELEC and ICETEL.

Additionally, the ICE Combo law would remove the Institute's restrictions on borrowing and investing and release it from its traditional obligations to the central government in terms of supplementing general revenues from the entity's surplus. Thus ICE would be permitted to act more like a private company itself.

Similarly, both ICETEL and ICELEC would be freed from restrictions on hiring and firing. In this way, they would achieve greater latitude in negotiating labor contracts. Nonetheless, workers would retain the protections against the loss of pay and benefits that they enjoyed under the previous ICE organization.

If transferred to one of the new entities envisioned under the reorganized ICE, employees would take with them all accumulated benefits.

Despite such measures, the new firms generated by the reorganization scheme would not be without government oversight. A new planning agency (Centro Nacional de Planificacion y Operacion de Electricidad, CENPO) would monitor the telecommunications and energy concessions as well as the marketing of electricity. Another agency, Autoridad Reguladora de las Telecomunicaciones (ARETEL), would control telecommunications. It would govern the distribution of cellular telephone bands and determine phone rates themselves. Provisions for protecting the interest of consumers is consistent with the warnings articulated by the World Bank when it points out that governments pay a high price in terms of support when "checks and balances" are absent; privatization without adequate regulation, accountability, and supervision of emerging private entities may result in failing efficiency and performance and open the process to corruption which would likely re-involve the government and undermine the program's legitimacy (World Bank, 1995). Sadly, the very president who articulated the ICE privatization proposal in 2000 and its accompanying governmental oversight, and who was installed in 2004 as the president of the Organization of American States, is currently serving a prison term for illegal activities during his administration, related to the privatization of Costa Rican government activities.

Opposition to the Combo Bill

Opposition to the ICE modernization proposal erupted throughout Costa Rica in March and April 2000. Opponents claimed that the law was a Trojan horse whose ultimate intent was the privatization of ICE itself. The chief objection to the bill was the allegation that it would eventually result in complete privatization of Costa Rica's utilities (Wolkoff, 2000). Moreover, ICE was superior to any private firm, since as a public company, the Institute could subsidize rates for those unable to pay for the basic services provided – something that private companies could not do, because of their for-profit character. This judgment received support from a National Assembly committee. It reported that the removal of subsidies would indeed cause local telephone and electricity rates to rise for residential consumers. Meanwhile rates for commercial and industrial users would decrease, since under the old ICE arrangement, their rates had been elevated to subsidize lower residential charges. Telephone tariffs for long distance calls would also fall.

Defenders of the bill countered such conclusions by pointing out that the law had set up a fund to maintain subsidies to selected residential users and for service in rural areas. In a nationally televised debate between Deputy Merino of the Partido Fuerza Democratica (PFD), who opposed the bill, and Assembly president Carlos Vargas of the governing Partido Unidad Social Cristiana

(PUSC), Vargas blamed the public disturbances on unions belonging to the leftist PFD. He alleged that it was part of the left's "strategy to destabilize the country" (2000).

For his part, Merino accused lawmakers favoring the bill of having sold their votes. He suggested a government investigation of the proponents' bank accounts. Vargas countered by accusing Merino and other PFD members of subservience to labor unions and of having sold out to them.

Such charges and counter-charges negatively affected the progress of the Combo's passage through the National Assembly. Even proponents of the new legislation concluded that the public simply did not sufficiently understand the proposal. One of these was Marco Vinicio Ruiz, head of the Cámara de Industrias de Costa Rica. Ruiz suggested to his 800 member businesses that they spend part of a workday explaining the bill to their employees. On March 24, Daniel Gallardo, leader of the PLN Assembly delegation, advised that his party members would withhold support in the second vote until the bill had been thoroughly explained to the demonstrators. With the concurrence of the PUSC leadership, he also suggested the Assembly correct certain aspects of the package, including issues of privatization, rates, rural service, and labor rights, and limitation of the degree of private-capital participation.

In response, the Rodriguez administration held that all such issues had already been addressed. Rodriguez himself called into question the sincerity of the protestors, referring to them as "professional agitators." They had systematically lied about the bill's content, he charged, adding that the protesters are "the same people who have gone on many marches." Accordingly, the president insisted that the bill be passed without alteration.

Nonetheless, widespread participation in the protests suggested that the issues surrounding the legislation extended far beyond ICE's privatization. Farmers objected to neo-liberal agricultural policy that removed tariff protection. Dockworkers were concerned about owed back pay. Public employees had taken to the streets because of salary increases promised but not received.

With all of this apparently in mind, political analyst Rodolfo Cerdas said the protests represented a rejection of the government's entire economic-development model. This was accompanied, he insisted, by a palpable fear among the middle class that they were falling into poverty.

Lack of honesty on the part of the Rodriguez administration also negatively affected the protestors. For example, the president had assured citizens that the bill would not have an adverse environmental impact. Nevertheless, it soon became clear that the legislation contained permission for private companies to exploit previously protected forests and other environmentally sensitive zones. Thus, the Environmental Ministry and ICE itself had provided authorization to locate plants within national parks (Wolkoff, 2000). There, according to the new legislation, ICELEC could build generating plants using geothermal energy, in exchange for setting aside two percent of its profits towards guaranteeing the parks' financial security. Similarly, plants using fossil fuels would have to pay one percent of their profits to the Fondo Nacional del Financiamiento Forestal (FONAFIFO) and to local reforestation projects. Such ostensibly pro-environmental provisions proved insufficient to deter environmentalists across Costa Rica from joining the anti-Combo protests in full force.

The multi-issue character of the March/April 2000 protests led even the conservative San Jose daily *La Nación* to conclude that the demonstrations reflected a generalized popular disaffection that could produce long-term political instability. The paper observed that the demonstrations stemmed from a lack of confidence in public officials due to past corruption scandals and to a conviction that government policies favor the rich and impoverish the majority.

After a week of protests, President Rodriguez accepted a proposal to set up a blue-ribbon commission to mediate his government's differences with unions and other protesting groups. However, Jorge Arguedas, coordinator of the ICE union Frente Interno de Trabajadores del Instituto Costarricense de Electricidad, warned that the commission was a maneuver to break up the protest movement. Nationwide protest against repeated police and National Guard interventions persisted until the Combo privatization initiative was put on permanent hold.

The Central American Free Trade Agreement

In addition to attempts to privatize the ICE from within the Costa Rican state apparatus, international forces have mounted concerted efforts in their own direction as well. Chief among these initiatives are the Free Trade Agreements represented by the Central American Free Trade Agreement (CAFTA), and the Free Trade Area of the Americas (FTAA). Both have originated from the Bretton-Woods Institutions and have been energized principally by the United States of America. The CAFTA would integrate all of Central America into a single trading body for the ultimate stated purpose of facilitating commerce between the region and the U.S.A., without governmentally imposed restrictions. It would be analogous to the accord implemented in 1994 between the United States, Canada, and Mexico, the North American Free Trade Agreement (NAFTA). The FTAA would similarly unite all countries of North and South America and the Caribbean.

A principal ingredient of all the trade pacts mentioned is privatization as understood in this study. And a chief component of the CAFTA's implementation in Costa Rica is the privatization of the ICE. The reasons advanced to justify the liberalization of ICE centralize the goals of service expansion, greater efficiency, increased productivity, lower service rates, modernization (e.g. more rapid inclusion of cellular phone technology), elimination of government bureaucracy, and discouragement of corruption. Examining each of these claims not only assists in the evaluation of the CAFTA relative to ICE, but also of arguments in favor of privatization in general, since, as we have seen, the goals just mentioned are precisely those invariably envisioned by proponents of the Washington Consensus.

Service Expansion

Nearly all sectors agree that the ICE should be modernized. Privatization advocates are correct when they point out that bureaucratic blockages presently prevent 40,000 customers from accessing the state service. Failures of this type in electricity and telecommunications provision are reportedly turning away prospective investors in a Costa Rican economy, which according to former President Rodriguez needs upwards of $4.5 billion over the next decade to meet consumer demand (Shadrin, 1992).

Nonetheless, 93.25 percent of Costa Rica's population currently enjoys electrical service, and 94 percent has access to telephone service. As shown in table 5.1, the country provides 31.60 telephone lines for every 100 inhabitants. Its closest competitor, Uruguay, has a public system similar to Costa Rica's. All the other countries listed have been privatized, but their figures after March 2004 are not available.

Table 5.1 Telephone Line Density Per 100 Inhabitants

Country	Telephone Lines*	March 2004**
Costa Rica	25	31.60
Uruguay	28	28.00
Chile	23	
Brazil	22	
Argentina	22	
Mexico	15	

* Source: International Telecommunications Union   ** Source: ICE

More telephone calls are completed from the United States to Costa Rica than to any other country in Latin America. These figures place Costa Rica in first place relative to telecommunications development among all Southern Hemisphere competitors (Fumero, 2004).

Table 5.2. Telephone Call Completions From the United States to Latin America

Country	Completion percent
Costa Rica	71.47
Chile	71.46
El Salvador	70.28
Guatemala	70.18
Venezuela	70.27
Brazil	68.59
Argentina	45

Source: AT&T, Costa Rica (June 12, 2003)

The point illustrated in table 5.2 is not that Costa Rica's percentages are that much larger than the other countries listed, but that the country is not only competitive with privatized phone systems, but actually outperforms them. Evidently, such considerations have drawn investors to the country. According to a recent report by the Harvard Institute for National Development, Costa Rica is the Latin American region's second most competitive country (Shadrin, 1992).

Greater Productivity and Efficiency

Costa Rica electrical and phone services rank among the most efficient and least expensive in Latin America. In both categories, the country currently ranks high among world leaders. The ICE has 5.35 employees per 1000 telephone service lines. The average in Latin America is 5.49. In Europe it is 6.10, and in Africa it is 12.82 (Fumero, 2004).

Table 5.3. Productivity Indices: Employees Per 100 Telephone Lines

Region	Employees
Costa Rica	5.35
The Americas	5.49
Oceania	5.75
Europe	6.10
Asia	6.37
Africa	12.82

Source: *Tiempos del Mundo*, 13/06/03. International Telecommunications Union 2001

Lower Service Rates

Here too Costa Rica's ICE is a world leader, with its service rates ranking among the lowest in the world. When the basic monthly rate in the country was $4 for a land-line phone, it was $19 in Panama, and $20 in Nicaragua.

Table 5.4. Residential Land Line Service Rate Comparision

Country	Basic Rate (U.S. $)	Minutes Alotted	Additional Minutes
Costa Rica	$4	60	0.01
Guatemala	N.D.		0.10
Honduras	N.D.		0.15
El Salvador	N.D.		0.12
Panama	$19	35	0.15
Nicaragua	$20	99	0.50

Source: AHCIET.

Additional minutes beyond basic allotment cost one cent in Costa Rica, ten cents in Guatemala, 12 cents in El Salvador, 15 cents in Honduras and Panama, and 50 cents in Nicaragua (Fumero, 2004).[4] Additionally, ICE's principles (based on the "solidaridad" concern for the common good) force it to extend its services to consumers who would otherwise be unable to pay. In fact, 84 percent of the Institute's fixed-rate clients are subsidized—from monies derived from the state's business sector, as well as by its mobile and international phone services (Fumero, 2004).

Modernization

Costa Rica is similarly efficient relative to modern cellular technology. When the basic monthly charge was $7 there, it was $12 in Panama, $15 in Honduras and El Salvador, $28 in Guatemala, and $30 in Nicaragua. Each additional minute in Cost Rica cost seven cents, while it cost 11 in Guatemala, 25 in Honduras, 27 in El Salvador, 35 in Nicaragua, and 45 cents in Panama. These rates were sufficient to rank Costa Rica third in the world (after the U.S. and Hong Kong) in per capita cellular phone consumption. Citizens in Costa Rica average 286 minutes per month, while those in the U.S. average 474, and those in Hong Kong, 350 (Fumero, 2004). Costa Rica is the only Central American country and one of only four Latin American countries listed by Merrill Lynch in the top 43 countries in terms of cellular phone usage.

Table 5.5. Per Person Cellular Phone Consumption
(Incoming and outgoing minutes per month)

Country	Minutes / Month	Country	Minutes/Month
USA	474	Egypt	162
Hong Kong	350	South Africa	158
Costa Rica	286	France	157
Korea	281	New Zealand	140
Canada	265	United Kingdom	137
Israel	254	Holland	126
India	249	Denmark	126
Finland	224	Russia	124
Nigeria	220	Austria	119
Singapore	219	Portugal	118
Malaysia	204	Chile	114
China	204	Switzerland	110
Prom Pond	196	Spain	98
Ireland	188	Hungary	98
Norway	170	Brazil	97
Australia	170	Argentina	92
Japan	164	Italy	15

Source: Merril Lynch, ICE.   *La Nación*, 01/22/04

Often the question of "bureaucracy" is framed as though governments were uniquely bureaucratic, while private enterprise typically avoids the delays, complications and unresponsive nature of institutions labeled pejoratively as "bureaucratic." Further investigation, however, reveals that many of the huge corporations like those vying to privatize various aspects of the ICE are themselves many-layered bureaucracies employing thousands of workers, with central control typically located continents away from the point of service. This raises a question central to the debate about "bureaucracy": which is preferable, a public bureaucracy whose members are periodically subject to review (by way of elections) from all citizens regardless of income level, or a private bureaucracy whose functionaries are principally responsive to customers—i.e. those able to pay. One could reasonably argue that the former (public bureaucracy) is at least more responsible to the larger general public need than would be private bureaucracy.

Discouragement of Corruption

Recent scandals involving at least three of Costa Rica's most recent presidents (and possibly the sitting president), in collusion with international businesses intent on privatizing the country's economy, have raised national consciousness in Costa Rica of the powerful corruptive influences inherent in the potential sale of state assets to private firms. President Miguel Angel Rodriguez, the Combo-Bill's principal advocate, is currently in prison (as mentioned above) and stands accused of corruption, accepting bribes, and of "illicit enrichment" from foreign companies (Barry, 2004, p.1). At least two of the accusations are intimately involved in ICE privatization measures. During Rodriguez's term in office, the French telecommunications firm, Alcatel, had been awarded a $149 million contract with the Institute. Allegedly Alcatel paid out a "prize" of $2.4 million for securing the contract. According to accusations, Rodriguez kept 60 percent of that prize and offered the other 40 percent to an ICE board member (Antonio Lobo), who later accused the ex-president of corruption (Barry). Rodriguez has been indicted for accepting a $100,000 payment from a Spanish firm, Inabensa, which had been commissioned to lay subterranean electrical cable throughout San Jose for the National Light and Power Company (CNFL). As we will see in subsequent chapters, charges have also been leveled against former president Rafael Angel Calderon, who is also serving time in a state prison in connection with the illegal use of influence within Costa Rica's Social Security agency, the Caja. Former president José María Figueres, who currently resides in Austria, has charges pending against him but has refused to return to Costa Rica. Allegations of similar nature have surfaced as well against Costa Rica's standing president, Abel Pacheco.

Conclusion

In summary, the analysis rendered here indicates that Costa Rica's ICE represents a case apart in the broad debate about privatization. This is because its "solidarity model" based on the principles of common good associated with the country's Second Republic (see chapter 3) have made it, along with Uruguay (which shares the solidarity model), the top two countries in terms of electricity and telecommunications development. That is, the model has given to Costa Rica the highest level of such services in Latin America (Fumero, 2004). Furthermore, the service has been made available and affordable for far more income-diversified customers than could possibly be reached by for-profit firms with their overriding concern of maximizing return to investors. Additionally, the consolidation of ICE electrical and telecommunication services under a single entity enables the Institute to optimize available resources. The two entities share physical plants, administration, equipment and vehicles. As a large enterprise, the Instituto Costarricense de Electricidad exercises economy of scale that lowers its own purchasing budget (Fumero).

Finally, as Fumero (2004) has observed:

> . . . the ICE is a means, the end being the provision of services to every Costa Rican home without consideration of place or income level. A development like that contemplated in the Free Trade Agreement and which would be defined in its accompanying legislation under the neo-liberal model imposed by the Agreement will not only terminate the ICE, it will end security, subsidies, the solidarity model, and our country's extraordinary level of service, which has been achieved here only after many decades of national effort (p.152).

---

1. Fumero (2004) describes the process of replacing ICE's guaranteed universal service (where the less affluent are subsidized by clients more able to pay) with a far less comprehensive arrangement in the following steps: (1) Private phone companies are allowed to enter the market in competition with ICE. (2) More affluent clients subscribe to the private companies' services, despite their higher rates, perhaps attracted by a higher-quality service. (3) In this way, the private companies skim the cream off the market's top and pocket the funds that formerly subsidized the economy's poorer sectors. (4) ICE is then forced to raise its rates, which less affluent users will not be able to pay; they drop out of the market. (5) With this transition, the rate difference between ICE and its competitors begin to narrow or disappear, which leads yet other more affluent clients to change their service to a private carrier. (6) Finally (and this has been the case in other Latin American countries), thousands will finds themselves unable to pay the higher rates, and the market will be left serving only the country's better-off citizens.

2. Oscar Arias, who eventually won the election, quipped that he'd prefer Nicaragua have a tenth commandant in its ruling junta (there were nine), since by his calculation each was worth $50 million in U.S. aid to Costa Rica.

3. Insight into the divisions concerning privatization among the day's political elite, even within the same party, was illustrated during an interview with Oscar Arias at his private residence 6 July 2000. This past reality has contemporary significance, since owing to a recent constitutional amendment, Oscar Arias is again able to run for president and is currently the leading candidate for 2006. During that interview, colleague Dr. Michael Rivage-Seul asked Dr. Arias about the policy of import substitution and why it was set aside. Arias commented that "the practice is 'crazy' because it ends up supporting inefficient local industries and causing consumers to pay the price." Rivage-Seul followed up, asking whether or not Costa Rica's economic "exceptionalism" (to the rest of Central America) seemed to be connected with the success of import substitution programs. "That is not true, sir," Arias replied. "In fact, the standard of living in Costa has risen dramatically since the end of the import substitution era. Thirty percent of Costa Ricans

lived below the poverty line when my administration began its work. Now the poverty figure has been reduced to 20 percent. In order to further reduce poverty, it is necessary to grow the economy. Investors must be welcomed. They are looking not only for low wages, but for high productivity and other elements such as low taxes, political stability, low inflation, good infrastructure, etc. All of this is part of the globalization/privatization debate; both, it is true, produce winners and losers. The losers are the poorly educated."

Oscar Arias's current position on free trade agreements (free trade is a topic of this chapter's concluding section) is consistent with his position while president from 1986-90 and the interview above in 2000. The stress within the party over divergent views of privatization has been largely responsible for the splits of 2005, the deepest divisions the party has experienced since its inception in 1948.

4. It should be noted that each of the phone systems of the countries mentioned here and depicted in table 5.4 have been privatized.

Chapter 6
Case Study of Costa Rican Privatization: La Caja Costaricense Del Seguro Social (CCSS) and El Instituto Nacional De Seguros (INS)

Introduction

Apart from affecting state-owned enterprises competing with private firms in the commodities sector of the economy, Costa Rica's trend towards privatization also seeks to incorporate state services such as social security and other types of insurance. These services differ from commodity production and sale in that Costa Rican insurance was never intended to generate income surplus. Rather, from the outset it was understood as a social service founded on the "solidarity model." As will be seen below, this model seeks to improve quality of life for the entire national population by having those with higher incomes subsidize identical services offered to those with fewer resources. To this end, the solidarity model provides services at or below cost to most consumers. Many solidarity supporters argue that it could be considered successful, even if, in the end, its enterprises never generated revenue surplus, and that even subsidies would be justified, if necessary.

This chapter examines two public enterprises of the type mentioned, the Caja Costarricense Del Seguro Social (CCSS, often referred to as the "Caja" or strong box) and the Instituto Nacional de Seguros (INS). The former represents the Costa Rican version of Social Security and covers universal health, unemploy-ment, disability, and retirement insurances. The INS offers supplemental insurance in these areas, and also covers mandatory auto insurance, support for fire departments, agricultural crop insurance, and property liabilities (Salas Picado, 1995).

What follows will offer a brief description of each program in terms of its history and founding legislation. Second, it will recount the efforts to privatize the programs, along with the countervailing endeavors of resistance movements. Each account will conclude by offering a preliminary analysis of the problematic aspects of privatizing health care and insurance in the Costa Rican context. That analysis will find summary and expansion in the study's concluding chapter.

Caja Costarricense del Seguro Social

The Caja Costarricense del Seguro Social was created by Law No. 17 of October 1943. It was incorporated into the National Constitution with the adoption of Article 73 and with the reform of article 77 of that same document. The period of its origin was characterized throughout Latin America by social movements whose working class protagonists sought to better their living standards and improve conditions in their places of employment (Salas Picado, 1995). Such movements succeeded in bringing about widespread reforms for workers and middle-class citizens in various countries throughout the region (Salazar, 1986). The particulars of these events in Costa Rica, especially those that took place during the Rafael Angel Calderón Guardia administration from 1940-1944, were laid out in chapter 2.

Prominent among these region-wide reforms was the extension of Social Security coverage to the entire Costa Rican population by 1971 (Salas Picado, 1995). With that, the state committed itself to insuring Costa Rican citizens' health, with special emphasis on occupational hazards, disabilities incurred "on the job," and risks from illness. As well, the new social legislation provided compensation to those who for various reasons lost their source of employment (Salas Picado). Preventive care was also built into the legislation that finally subsumed all the country's hospitals into a single system (Law 5349, 1973).

The CCSS system was oriented not only towards the good of the entire Costa Rican society but towards development of an internal market in health and insurance. In terms of employment alone, the CCSS's impact was significant. In 1989 its labor force numbered 21,428 (Salas Picado, 1995). The Institute's economic impact eventually came to represent about 7 percent of Costa Rica's gross domestic product. With such resources at stake, the CCSS provoked intense debate about the most efficient use of its assets. It has also stimulated great interest on the part of private firms anxious to attain access to the institution's multimillion dollar budget. With these characteristics, the CCSS came to be regarded as the "crown jewel" of the state social system. Since changes in this basic system would be seen as carrying profound implications for the entire Costa Rican society, there is a sense within Costa Rica that any alterations would need the consensus of the entire population (Salas Picado).

Privatization Efforts

Efforts at privatizing the CCSS have surfaced and resurfaced almost from the beginning, though mostly in quiet and unobtrusive ways – often in the form of "pilot projects" (Salas Picado, 1995). Privatization measures intensified, however, from 1978 to 1982 in the midst of Costa Rica's severe economic crisis. Administrative structures in both the governmental and CCSS facilities proved slow in responding to the changing economic and health care needs of Costa Rica. Currently CCSS privatization efforts take the form of modifications introduced by the Central American Free Trade Agreement (CAFTA), which seeks extension of intellectual property rights connected with medicine.

Caja Privatization 1978-1982

Attempts to privatize aspects of the CCSS from 1978-1982 surfaced when threats from old infectious diseases such as malaria, tuberculosis, polio, and dengue fever had greatly diminished. As a result, life expectancy for Costa Ricans had been extended. Challenges presented by this emerging situation were compounded with the appearance of new maladies, including cancer, heart disease, and hypertension. At the same time, extreme budget constraints exacerbated by the national economic crisis limited options at the disposal of administrative personnel.

To cope with these altered situations, the initial administrative response (though seemingly illogical) was to add new health workers to the state's payroll. Thus between 1978 and 1982, the number of such employees rose from 16,000 to 23,000 – all to service the same number of hospital beds. A second contradictory response, beginning with the "Hundred Days Plan" during the Monge administration (1982-1986) was to introduce austerity measures. These greatly restricted overtime for health care workers, substituted time off for wages in particular cases, and even enforced new limits on the issuance of materials such as pencils, paper, soap, and towels (Salas Picado, 1995). Still, even the most extreme of these measures met with little worker opposition, since they were understood as policies needed to "save the CCSS."[1]

However, union members mounted opposition when it became apparent that privatization measures were in the works. Such policies became clear first with a plan to privatize laundries in Hospital Mexico and the Hospital of Cartago. At this point, union members began articulating their understanding of privatization as "replacement of workers and the loss of labor rights" (Salas Picado, p.122). With the extension of this understanding across the CCSS's employees, early privatization efforts were halted.

Objections from labor, however, did not prove successful in blocking the emergence of a subsequent "Program for the Transfer of Activities," under the aegis of MIDEPLAN. The alleged reasons for privatization included the continued inability of the CCSS's administration to resolve the institution's burgeoning problems, the persistent deterioration of services, loss of morale among the workforce (especially among physicians), and the channeling of resources towards inappropriate projects (e.g. housing) (Salas Picado, 1995). Accordingly, fourteen activities were identified as transferable to the private sector. They included, once again, laundry services, but also departments such as maintenance, pharmaceutical services, clothing and eyeglass manufacture, and dietetics (MIDEPLAN, 1985). With these particular changes, some 2,500 public employees were scheduled to lose their positions. But even this figure was only half the proposed eliminations scheduled by President Monge (Salas Picado, 1995). In the end, about 2,000 workers were dropped from the Republic's payroll by way of attrition and early retirement.

The way was prepared for further reductions in the labor force by the creation of the "Program for the Study of Organizational Alternatives for the Workers of the Costa Rican CCSS." This program was directed by a commission composed of the directors of the medical, administrative, and financial divisions, as well as coordinators of human resources and technical consultation. The commission sponsored seminars through the CCSS's Center for Training and Development. Labor union speakers charged that these events were wrongly used to promote the transfer of services to the private sphere. Union representatives also charged that privatization efforts destabilized the country's labor markets, threatened labor unions, involved risky investment schemes, and did not adequately compensate workers who lost jobs as a result of downsizing measures inherent in privatization plans (Salas Picado, 1995).

Despite labor union objections, privatization plans moved ahead. Such efforts, however, were not directed at the entire institution, but distinct activities under its aegis. Health services strictly understood comprised a main target (Salas Picado, 1995). Two cases of such privatization are particularly instructive, the clinics at Pavas and Barva. Both represent privatization efforts offered by co-ops closely associated with the CCSS, opposed by labor unions, but approved by local communities as obviating the administrative delays and inefficiencies often associated with State-run institutions.

The Pavas Clinic is an autonomous medical cooperative. As such, it is a private enterprise designed and operated by a group of physicians. The doctors themselves come from the CCSS or Ministry of Health. The clinic's administrative personnel, however, have been selected and trained by the co-op itself. These administrators have been especially careful to solicit input from community members whose means are extremely limited and whose medical needs tend to be of the most basic nature. As a result of this solicitude, support for the clinic within the Pavas community has been strong, despite strong opposition from labor unions associated with the CCSS (Salas Picado, 1995).

Under these arrangements, doctors at the Pavas Clinic receive salaries superior to those determined strictly by market forces. Procedures at the clinic have also managed to obviate the standard administrative delays experienced in State-run facilities. Likewise, material resources within the clinic have been more quickly obtained and made available to clients (Salas Picado, 1995).

The Barva Clinic is very similar in organization and administration to the clinic at Pavas. Barva, however, is distinguished by its method of remunerating its medical personnel. It pays them according to the number of patients each physician services (Salas Picado, 1995). According to a study conducted by the Center for Training and Development (CECADE), in October 1987, this method of payment in no way lowered the quality of service offered in the clinic (CECADE, 1988).

CCSS Privatization under CAFTA

The most comprehensive attempts at privatizing the Costa Rican insurance monopoly are represented by the proposed Central American Free Trade Agreement (CAFTA). As earlier noted, this free trade arrangement between the United States and Central America is currently the object of intense debate within the country. The agreement would privatize the country's insurance monopoly according to the following steps:

1. Immediately upon approval of the CAFTA by the Costa Rican National Assembly, the insurance market would be opened to insurance providers from other countries, without their being permitted to establish offices in Costa Rica itself.

2. On January 1, 2007, an Insurance Regulatory Agency would be established.

3. From July 1, 2007, private insurance companies would be able to open offices in Costa Rica, but only for the sale of "business" insurance.

4. From January 1, 2008, private companies offering all types of insurance (except working persons' compensation and automobile insurance) would be able to open offices in Costa Rica.

5. From January 1, 2011, private companies offering all types of insurance, including working persons' compensation and automobile insurance, would be able to open offices in Costa Rica (Unión del Personal, 2004).

A Negotiator's Evaluation

Germán Serrano Pinto, the former executive president of the INS and former minister of Labor and Social Security in Costa Rica, offers an authoritative and cogent evaluation of attempts to privatize his country's insurance monopoly. Serrano played a leading role in CAFTA negotiations. He subsequently reported unfavorably to Costa Rica's president about the treaty's impact on the state's 80-

year-old insurance system. Shortly thereafter, he was dismissed from his post (Serrano, 2004). Serrano summarizes his objections as follows:

> . . . the general conclusion we draw is that (CAFTA insurance provisions) are the product of an hermetic process of negotiation, characterized by technical ignorance on the part of the negotiators. As a result, they have accepted accords that seriously threaten not only the Costa Rican insurance market by opening it indiscriminately to cross-border business, but also our own social security (by including in the treaty social or "solidarity" insurances) and to an important degree the very economy of our country. Under the treaty, not only does our economy lose a large portion of the profit produced by commercial insurance but also savings deposits and premiums in our banks, along with the flight of capital produced under both rubrics. In addition, the treaty does not require reciprocity from all signatories, it establishes absurd and even fatal deadlines, and it de-emphasizes benefit of the general consumer as well as the prerequisites necessary for optimal supervision and regulation. Accordingly, the only clear and fitting recommendation to be made is the renegotiation of the treaty's text, at least as far as the topic of insurance is concerned, in order to address the shortcomings just indicated (p.109).

With these words, Serrano advances six basic criticisms of privatization plans as affecting the insurance industry and as framed in the CAFTA texts:

> 1. Costa Rican negotiators in the process are basically ill-prepared, and hence have been led into accepting a text that takes advantage of their ignorance. Insurance, Serrano observes, is a highly complicated topic and demands transparency and participation by experts and by all affected parties – including consumers and sectors of the economy indirectly but crucially involved in the momentous changes embraced by the treaty (see point 4 below) (Serrano, 2004).
>
> 2. Absence of expert negotiators, along with lack of transparency, and widespread participation has resulted in a treaty that prioritizes commercial benefit over consumer welfare. The fact that treaty provisions open the industry before official oversight is established opens the door to irresponsible insurance practices for which ordinary Costa Ricans will end up paying the price (Serrano, 2004). Accordingly, a well-planned program of consumer education is required to protect clients from an industry Serrano characterizes as "voracious" (p. 54). The insurance supervisory agency, Serrano urges, should be established at least six months before any privatization measures take effect (p. 55).
>
> 3. The treaty's implementation schedule is artificially rushed. To begin with, the CCSS operation was to be excluded altogether from CAFTA negotiations, since Costa Rican negotiators had declared themselves less interested in discussing privatization plans that included the CCSS. Consequently, it was only at the eleventh hour that negotiators even put it on the table (Serrano, 2004). Secondly, though the implementation of the CAFTA privatization program promises to follow a step-by-step schedule, the timetable is not gradual enough. It sets artificial deadlines that effectively rush through a program whose im-

plementation dates are predetermined, even before the treaty's approval. This means that the treaty clock is running even before official approval is given. No other parties to the CAFTA were subject to such narrow timetables. Serrano (2004) asks, why establish activation dates before the treaty has been approved? In any case, he observes, at least five more years—preferably ten—are required before the complete privatization of the insurance industry as proposed by the Treaty under negotiation.

4. The CAFTA agreements threaten not only the insurance industry, but also highly-prized citizen guarantees including health care, retirement, and workers' compensation. It thus overlooks Costa Rica's unique social heritage, which protects workers' rights—as opposed to other Central American parties to the CAFTA that have long histories of worker exploitation and deprivation of labor rights. By ignoring and nullifying the achievements of Costa Rican workers, the CAFTA pact threatens to reduce them to the status traditionally inflicted on other regional labor forces (Serrano, 2004).

5. The CAFTA undermines Costa Rica's national economy, actually promoting capital flight by depriving the economy of reserve deposits from insurance transactions, as well as deposits resulting from insurance premiums themselves. Deposits from the insurance industry provide the Costa Rican nation with an important funding source for various social and economic projects. Replacing that funding source would mean either a reduction in services or a rise in taxes (Serrano, 2004). Additionally, the insurance business brings with it important multiplier effects in terms of local employment and the development of local sub-economies.

6. The agreement is not characterized by reciprocity, since it binds Costa Rica to obligations not embraced by other parties to the CAFTA pact. Thus, for instance, though Costa Rica is required to unreservedly open its insurance market to branches of foreign companies seeking to locate there, a corresponding opportunity is not necessarily given Costa Rican insurance agencies in other signatory countries. Also, even when allowed to open branches in other countries, Costa Ricans themselves can be obliged to fulfill residency requirements or even to become citizens of the country in question. No such obligations are imposed by the treaty in Costa Rica (Serrano, 2004)

Serrano (2004) adds that privatization as advanced in the CAFTA impinges on Costa Rican sovereignty. It makes permanent rules which at some future date may need revision for the sake of national welfare but which Costa Ricans will find themselves powerless to change. The relevant regulation found troublesome to Serrano would commit Costa Rica to extend:

> . . . to financial institutions of the party of the second part and to the investments of investors of that party in financial institutions, a treatment no less favorable than that extended, in similar circumstances, to its own financial institutions and to the invest-ments of its own investors in financial institutions,

with respect to establishment, acquisition, expansion, administration, conduct, operation, and sale or other form of disposition of financial institutions and investments (Unión del Personal, 2004, p. 167).

That is, Costa Rica would not be able to give preferential treatment to any investors or financial institutions, including insurance companies, regardless of their nature, intentions, or promised comparative benefit to Costa Rican citizens, natural environment, or any other aspect of national life. In virtue of the CAFTA, the Costa Rican National Assembly could be guilty of a treaty violation, even were it to offer favorable treatment to a company whose policies were judged to be of more national benefit than those of any competitor. In effect, then, the CAFTA's privatization plan in general, and its provisions for the insurance industry in particular, surrender a portion of the country's independence to external bodies which can make decisions contrary to the will of the people and their elected representatives (Serrano, 2004).

In view of his objections, Serrano (2004) recommends first of all, that insurance not be included in the CAFTA pact—i.e. that Costa Rica's insurance industry not be privatized, at least according to the CAFTA requirements. If such exclusion proves impossible, Serrano's fallback position is that a request for further study be honored. In any case, disclaimers must be incorporated into any version of the treaty specifically protecting Costa Rica's national sovereignty.

Medical Insurance and Intellectual Property

Once the insurance monopoly has been broken, another set of issues intimately related to privatization of health insurance surfaces. Chief among them is the set of issues related to patents and to Trade Related Intellectual Property (TRIPs) as they touch the medical services offered by the Caja. As defined by Vandana Shiva (2001), patents "are an exclusive right granted to an inventor to make, produce, distribute, and sell a patented product or use patented processes" (p. 11).[2] TRIPS represent an attempt by the GATT (General Agreement on Tariffs and Trade) and WTO (World Trade Organization) to extend U.S.-style intellectual property rights to all signatory governments and members of the Agreement and Organization (Shiva, 2001). As will be seen, both of these terms, patents and TRIPs, play central roles in the world-wide debate about the privatization of knowledge in general and of medical formulae in particular. In controversy about the Caja and privatization, intellectual property and patents affect the costs of medicine, which, in turn, affects the budget of Costa Rica's health care system, which in turn influences judgments about the viability of the entire system.

Patents have a long history of development in Europe and reflect a particular approach to knowledge. *Litterae patentes* were originally instruments of entitlement. In the sixth century C.E., as indicated by the Latin name, they were "open letters" in the sense of charters or official documents. First issued by European monarchs, Patent Letters announced the conferral of rank, privilege, rights, and titles on the beneficiary. In particular, documents gave their bearers the authorization to conquer foreign lands and colonies on behalf of the conferring sovereign and to establish trade monopolies in his or her name. At the end of the 15th century, Christopher Columbus bore such "patents" from Ferdinand and Isabella of Spain, when they sent him to what they thought would be India. The letters established beforehand Columbus's right to "discover and conquer" (the phrases occur seven times in the letters) all "islands and mainlands"—thus granting the Admiral of the Ocean Fleet the potential right to own India on behalf of the Spanish crown (Shiva, 2001).

Patents were not consistently associated with intellectual property until the Renaissance, when they first appear in Italy, and shortly thereafter in England. They granted exclusive monopolies which forbade the use of the device in question without the patent-holder's permission. That permission had to be granted, however, in exchange for "reasonable" royalties. In this first form, patents licensed the use of devices and processes that were unknown in a particular jurisdiction, even though they might have been used elsewhere. In their words, patents were not issued for new and original inventions only. Both imports and previous inventions could be patented (Shiva, 2001).[3]

It was by the importation and patenting of previous inventions and processes that both Great Britain and the United States industrialized. In the 14th century, for example, England found itself lagging behind its European competitors in the early stages of the Industrial Revolution. To remedy the situation, the British lured skilled craftsmen and artisans from foreign countries to introduce apprentices to the mysteries of their arts. Part of the enticement was the assurance, in the form of patents, that the skilled émigrés would be protected from competition coming from their students for a period of seven to fourteen years. Since it normally took seven years for apprentices to learn a craft, this meant on the one hand, that one or two generations of trainees would be technically prepared under the tutelage of the guest artisan, and, on the other, that the instructor himself would enjoy monopoly protection from his students for seven to fourteen years (Shiva, 2001).

Encouragement of technology transfer, rather than its prevention, was also the motivation behind the first patent laws passed in the United States. As Shiva (2001) puts it:

> The early US patent laws, like European laws, were for introducing new methods that were unknown in the US but practiced elsewhere. They were not related to inventiveness, only to the fact that the practice was not being undertaken within the US and hence could be treated as 'presumed to be unknown.' Present-day states in the US started to pass laws to protect monopolies, often based on use of imported technologies and methods of manufacture. Salt patents were among the first to be granted in the colonies. For example, in 1641, Samuel Winslow was granted an exclusive right to make salt (p. 17).

The U.S. Patent Act of 1952 reaffirmed the understanding of patents as grantable for devices and processes previously unknown or unused in Federal territories, regardless of their use elsewhere. The Patent Act, then, provides for patents to be granted for existing knowledge and assisted the process of developed-world industrialization and the transfer of technology from one country to another, and protected the use of that technology from foreign competition. (This could even include competition from those who had originated the devices and processes in the first place.)

According to Vandana Shiva (2001), two tendencies of the modern industrialized economy have shifted the understanding of patents from instruments to transfer previously existing technology to devices for the prevention of such transfer in order to protect those claiming rights to an "invention." The first was the stagnation of industrialized economies in the late 1970s. The economic imperative to "grow the economy" made it necessary for economically developed countries to seek new markets. Second, the traditionally industrialized countries found their roles as manufacturing leaders in decline. Both tendencies caused a shift in the production priorities of the industrialized north, especially of the United States. Consequently, its economy shifted from industrial production to the production of knowledge and services (Shiva).

For such an economy to succeed, however, it was necessary to strengthen intellectual property rights and to extend the U.S. understanding of such rights to the world economy in which it moves. Countries trading with the U.S. would, in effect, be accountable to the laws that already applied in the U.S. Inventions granted patents in California would have to be respected in Costa Rica and vice-versa. Under CAFTA, the ability to patent imported technologies would be eliminated, and sovereign control over inventions introduced within ones own borders would be reduced or eliminated.

Patenting Medicines in Costa Rica

There are three standard rationales for the privatization of knowledge through patent protection of intellectual property rights (IPRs) in general and for the privatization and protection of medical knowledge and formulae in particular. All are rooted in the same "western" approach to knowledge and its ownership. (This in recognition of the existence of varying starting points and the relativity of ownership within different cultures.)

The first reason for IPRs' protection by patents holds that IPRs are essential to free trade and to free market competition. With the failure of "historic socialism," this is commonly taken as a self-evident good, often associated with the spread of democracy. The second reason is that competitiveness will lower the costs of medicine for the consuming public, while raising medicine's quality. In this way the common good will be served by the privatization of medical knowledge protected by patents. The third reason is that patent protection will enable creative firms to recoup their tremendous research and development costs. It is generally recognized, even by opponents of IPRs, that development of new medical products costs tens of millions of dollars, as do the government-mandated tests of such products before they can be made available to the consumer (Weissman, 2004).

Patents and Market Theory

Opponents of privatization and patent protectionism relative to medical knowledge point out that such measures intentionally contradict free market principles rather than advance them. Their intention, however, is to do so only temporarily. Thus Weissman (2004) observes:

> Patents have as their central intention the stimulation of innovation and constitute a kind of contradictory parenthesis within liberal economic theory itself. That theory supposes that market competition is the best way to maximize social benefit and to guarantee the best use of productive resources. For their part, patents constitute a concession of a monopoly on the part of the State to an innovator for a period of twenty years, during which time the patent owner has the exclusive right to produce and market the product of his innovation. (p. 105)

Here Weissman indicates that patents' departure from free-market competition is only provisional and temporary. Their purpose is to stimulate and reward innovation. Once the period of 20 years has passed, the patent dissolves and competition is reintroduced to stimulate product quality and lower prices. However, Weissman indicates that the CAFTA would make provision for firms holding these temporarily exclusive rights to extend their patents' life beyond a 20-year span and even to make permanent the monopoly the patents grant.[4]

Patents, Prices and Product Quality

Opponents of patent-protected IPRs allege that patents' reduction of competition leads inevitably to higher prices and reduced product quality and innovation. This they claim would be especially true, since, according to proposed CAFTA regulations, governments would be prevented from issuing "Obligatory Licenses" to firms producing generic drugs as alternatives to higher priced patented products. Obligatory licenses permit governments to award patents to third parties (private firms, government agencies, etc.) on medical products to which second parties already hold patents (Weissman, 2004). These licenses have been a tool frequently used by governments to reduce prices on medicines necessary to respond to the medical needs of local citizens.

> Provisions of trade agreements, which delay the introduction of competition of generic drugs, also delay the benefits obtainable through reduced prices and broadened accessibility. This has a lethal effect in the case of vital medicines such as anti-viral drugs and reduces quality of life for patients when it is a case of necessary medicines that in some cases are indispensable (Wesissman, 2004, p.113).

Without the tool of "Obligatory Licenses," the prices of medicines predictably remain high—often 50 times higher than prices found in a genuinely competitive market—or in economies where prices of medicine are subject to government controls. Canada represents the latter case. Its lower prices are responsible for U.S. citizens seeking ways to import Canadian medicines into their own country (Weissman, 2004).

Lack of competition encouraged by patents of ever-longer duration may well discourage innovation, which has often been based on free exchange of information, rather than on the monopolization of information, and on the protection of that monopoly (Shiva, 2001). Additionally, opponents take exception to the theory of patents' identification of motivation to innovate with profit incentive alone. They point to ample evidence of scholars and scientist (especially in university and public research systems [and some also refer to work among indigenous or traditional peoples]) who have found incentive for their work and been successful in creating valuable medical breakthroughs in the absence of likely profit.

Weissman (2004) similarly addresses the argument that patents lead to greater benefit for the consumer in terms of product accessibility for more consumers. Patents, he argues, not only contradict free market theory in terms of competition, they also do so by prioritizing producers' self-interest over that of consumers. He refers to:

> . . . a social tension between the interests of patent owners and those of consumers. This contradiction acquires a special ethical dimension when pharmaceuticals are in question, given that monopoly control on the part of patent owners denies access to essential medicines to immense social sectors that depend on those medicines to improve their quality of life, or even to keep them from dying. (p. 105)

Patents as Reimbursement for Research and Development

As indicated earlier, patent protectionism rewards risk-taking firms for their investments. Noted as well was the fact that many on both sides of the privatization debate acknowledge that the protection granted by patents is evoked by the huge expenses pharmaceutical firms incur in their research and development efforts.

The counter argument submits that corporations often buy patents from public sector institutions or small inventors (and in some cases from traditional societies). These opponents point to the example that 92 per cent of cancer drugs discovered between 1955 and 1992 were developed with funding from the US government. Patents for cancer drugs, however, are owned almost exclusively by large private companies. (Shiva, 2001)

Conclusions

This review of the efforts to privatize the Caja Costarricense Del Seguro Social, has emphasized IPR provisions within CAFTA. The Tratado de Libre Comercio (Free Trade Agreement or TLC), is the most hotly debated political-economic topic in Costa Rica today. And though Costa Rica's system of National Health care was poked at by privatizors during the 1980, and implicated in the Structural Adjustment initiatives of the 1990s, it is the CAFTA and IPRs that would have the greatest impact on the public/private debate in relation to the Caja. The following conclusions are suggested:

1. The patent system of privatizing medical knowledge threatens to undermine Costa Rica's Caja system of health insurance by extending the life span of patents and removing the country's ability to issue Obligatory Licenses.

2. Such privatization would undoubtedly greatly increase the cost of health care in Costa Rica and undermine one of the core objectives of the Caja (and arguably a central rationale for free market reforms.) If food and medicine are available only at a price that is beyond the reach of [the common] people, the basic promise of the patent system as a contract that encourages private gain so that public goods can be provided is undermined. When the consumer's rights to food and health are undermined, there is no ground for granting patents, since patents are supposed to be a balance between the interests of producers on the one hand and consumers on the other (Shiva, 2001, p. 38).

3. Privatization of knowledge in the field of medicine at the expense of public benefit has been deemed unconstitutional by a number of Costa Rican authorities.

4. Alterations in the social, political, and economic context warrant reassessment of even the most revered institutions within a given culture. That is, new conditions within Costa Rica may require changes in inherited models. For the sake of stability (and the common good), there must be provisions for those who experience exclusion as a result (Salas Picado, 1995).

5. Relative to health care, privatization initiatives have tended to lack coherent strategy for coping with changed conditions. The intent to privatize is clear. However, particular programs have been perceived as being imposed in a haphazard, top-down manner and with a one-size-fits-all formulation. Implementation is often opportunistic, rather than holistic with strong reliance on assessment of local community needs.

6. Physicians stand to benefit economically from privatization of medical services. Additionally, the process of privatization offers them more decision-making powers and administrative options. They therefore tend to support the transference of medical services from state to private hands (Salas Picado, 1995).

7. Labor organizations almost invariably oppose privatization efforts. In Costa Rica, the nurses' union presented low-key opposition, while UNDECA was more demonstrative and vocal in its hostility (Salas Picado, 1995). In neither case, however, have unions demonstrated a clear vision of alternatives for coping with the deficiencies of State-run health care services. Instead, union strategy has appeared to be that of "extinguishing fires," or responding to crises threatening the self-interest of their members. Unions have underwritten the institution without adequately addressing its problems.

8. As shown especially in the case of the Pavas Clinic, community involvement plays a key role in determining whether or not privatization is a good idea. In Pavas, community members favored privatization despite strong opposition from unions claiming to represent the best interests of working people.[5] Community involvement might even go so far as to involve genuine plebiscite.

9. Privatization is not simply a matter of turning over health care facilities to domestic or international private corporations. As indicated in both Pavas and Barva, it can also take the form of health care cooperatives, which were responsive to community needs.

10. There is evidence that indicates that privatization of the type exemplified in Pavas and Barva can improve the quality of service offered by health care institutions—especially in relation to support services (Salas Picado, 1995).

11. As a result, blanket opposition to privatization efforts tends to lack credibility (Salas Picado, 1995).

12. Analysis of efforts to privatize the CCSS over the past 25 years strongly support the argument that privatization is not a purely technical matter. It requires holistic analysis and careful examination of the social, political, economic, and institutional context in which it develops.

El Instituto Nacional de Seguros

The Instituto Nacional de Seguros (INS) was established in Costa Rica according to Law No. 12 of October 30th, 1924.[6] It was intended as an expression of social responsibility for all Costa Ricans and foreign residents within the country. From its beginning the INS was a non-profit arrangement intended to foster social welfare rather than achieve market goals of capital accumulation. More specifically, the INS, from the outset, represented an intentional method of wealth redistribution for Costa Rican nationals. As is the case with the Caja, INS was founded as a "solidarity system," which would use profits from low risk liabilities to compensate for higher-risk contracts (Unión, 2004). In the words of Gerardo Fumero (2004):

> . . . private sector insurance accepts only the most lucrative risks, while a State insurance system uses the most lucrative securities to subsidize insurance risks of greater social utility, such as those originating from on-the-job injuries, retirement, or pensions. (p. 154)

Anticipating Fumero's observation, Tomas Soley Guel, Costa Rica's secretary of housing in 1924, expressed the founding perception of the INS in this way:

> Insurance is a problem of human solidarity. As a state monopoly, it amounts to a mutual fund intended as a preventive measure to protect the country's population by means of establishing solidarity among its inhabitants.
>   As an insurer, the state obviates the deficiencies of private insurance businesses, because it understands insurance for what it truly is, viz., a problem of human solidarity.(Fumero, 2004).

INS Founding Principles

The original justifications for the INS state monopoly 80 years ago remain the same today. They include:

1. Avoidance of capital flight by private companies that are normally reluctant to reinvest their profits in the Costa Rican economy.[7]

2. Avoidance of the formation of de facto monopolies that escape the moderating disciplines of free competition.

3. The establishment of a de facto insurance monopoly both as a social service and as an income source for the State.[8]

4. The broadening of insurance provisions as widely and to as many population sectors as possible—an expansion unlikely to be provided by a private sector concerned principally with for-profit activities rather than social service.

5. Avoidance of the violation of the "good faith principle" contravened by such practices as intentional destruction of insured property by fire, declarations of false information, and other forms of deception that threaten to foster among Costa Ricans a culture of corruption.

6. The thwarting of the practices of private insurance companies that declare
bankruptcy or simply disappear when faced with extraordinary liabilities such
as those resulting from catastrophic occurrences (Fumero, 2004).

These six justifications recognize insurance as a natural monopoly whose supporters believe that the probability for abuse increases when located in private
sector hands. Chief among the abuses to be avoided are price gouging resulting
from the naturally monopolistic character of the industry, capital flight depriving
the internal economy of billions of dollars in revenue, denial of responsibility
and compensation for catastrophic events, avoidance of insurance coverage for
high risk clients—especially those most in need of insurance, and the fostering of
a culture of dishonesty and corruption. Such liabilities, INS founders judged,
were best circumvented by a state monopoly of insurance.

Types of INS Coverage

From its inception, Costa Rica's state insurance monopoly covered (a) working
person's compensation; (b) mandatory auto insurance; (c) health care and medical services; (d) support for fire departments; (e) harvest insurance; and (f) property liabilities (Fumero, 2004).

Workers' Compensation

Workers' Compensation in Costa Rica covers all Costa Rican workers and foreign residents in cases of injury or illness, even in cases where the workers in
question are not in fact covered by their employers' policies (Fumero, 2004).
Historically, lack of coverage by employers occurred frequently, despite Article
73 of the Costa Rican Constitution, which instructs: " . . . insurance against professional risks will be the exclusive esponsibility of employers and will be governed by special regulations."
    This was reinforced on March 9, 1982, by the "Occupational Risk Law"
(No. 6727): "All employers, whether public or private are obligated to insure
their workers against on-the-job risks through the National Insurance Institute."
    In the same law, Article 201 mandates:

> For the benefit of workers, insurance against occupational risks in every field
> of endeavor is obligatory, universal, and compulsory. Any employer who does
> not insure workers will be liable before his or her workers as well as before the
> insuring agency for all medical and health care expenses, for rehabilitation, and
> cash payments as determined under this Title, and as mandated by the said in-
> surance provider.

Under such provisions, in 2003 alone 182,734 Costa Rican workers received medical attention as first-time patients, as recipients of follow-up care, for diagnostic observation in hospitals, and for similar medical needs. For these services, the Department of Occupational Risks invested almost $6 billion in the Costa Rican economy.

With such legal codifications and occupational needs in mind, the Department of Business Regulations mandated under article 268 of Title IV in the Labor Code, the improvement of occupational conditions and environment. As such, the Department offered workers and their employers the following services:

1. A program of general information in the form of manuals, pamphlets, and electronic media touching such matters as order, cleanliness, and preventive intervention in the workplace. For purposes of its credibility, this informational program received State certification in 2003, under the ISO-9000 standard.[9]

2. An annual training program for business leaders in matters of hygiene and security.[10]

3. A program of consultation and preventive intervention (against occupational risks).

4. A program of hygienic services for the evaluation of physical and chemical contaminants.[11]

5. Publication of the magazine, *Prevention*, the only glossy publication of its kind published in Costa Rica, with distribution at no cost to the reader.

6. An Internet Web site with full-text publication of regulations, with links to certified sites for purposes of related information discovery (Fumero, 2004).

Automobile Insurance

The law governing automobile insurance in Costa Rica was passed on September 13, 1976. Thus Article 42 of Law No. 5930, the Land Traffic Law, "Establishes obligatory insurance for automotive vehicles that operate within the country" (Fumero, 2004).

Costa Rican motorists meet their insurance fee requirement each year when they secure the right to put their vehicle on the road by acquiring their vehicle "registration stickers," referred to in Costa Rica as the marchamo. This entitles them to one million colones of coverage (two thousand dollars) for each accident in which they are involved, though, in cases of serious accidents, the payment can be higher. Motorists may also buy additional coverage, including collision, by paying supplemental fees (Fumero, 2004). The cost, however, for the basic coverage secured by the marchamo is about $20 per year, though this increases relative to the value of the vehicle.

In 2002, a total of 16,428 insurance claims were filed on behalf of 20,963 injured persons and 254 traffic fatalities. In 2003 the Required Automobile Insurance office paid out a total of $48 million to claimants (Fumero, 2004).

INS Health care and Medical Services

Costa Rican medical insurance covers victims of accidents at work or on the road, as well as those suffering from other types of illnesses. The system is considered one of the most effective in Latin America. It provides the benefit of modern medical technology, including access to the most advanced medicines, and to highly trained personnel.[12] It offers immediate attention to those requiring primary care, with consultation of medical specialists guaranteed within three days, although immediately in cases of emergency. Operations must be scheduled three weeks in advance, although they can be arranged in a week or less in cases of emergency (Fumero, 2004).[13]

Support for Firefighters

The Costa Rican insurance monopoly is responsible for the maintenance of the country's firefighting corps. Like the health care services just reviewed, the Costa Rican Fire Department is considered one of the best services of its kind in Latin America (Fumero, 2004). In the year 2003 alone, the INS contributed more than 6 billion colones ($12 million) to this highly effective fire fighting service.

Harvest Insurance

Costa Rica's crop insurance provisions were established on November 10, 1969, when Law No. 4461 was passed. The provisions were universalized on September 27, 1976, through the passage of Law No. 5932, the Law of Full and Universal Crop Insurance. That law adopted the use of a table indicating the types of crops insurable for each region of the country. Crops are underwritten for the amount the insured farmer has invested in the sowing of his crop.

Costa Rica is one of the few countries in the world to offer harvest insurance of this type to its farmers. Such service is considered excessively risky for private insurance agencies. Consequently, crop insurance in other countries is commonly available only to those with incomes substantial enough to meet the high premiums exacted.[14] By contrast, Costa Rica offers low-cost crop insurance to all farmers following its social solidarity principle, whereby surpluses generated in one part of the INS system are transferred to those with deficits. Over the last three years alone, the Costa Rican Crop Insurance System, through the

Commission of Farmers and Ranchers, has enabled farmers to pay their debts through subsidies amounting to 16,579,000,000 colones, or $33 million (Fumero, 2004).

Property Insurance

In Costa Rica, the INS offers no special insurance for commercial properties or ventures. Rather, businesses are insured in the same way that homes and other properties are covered. The system of coverage centralizes the social solidarity principle. Thus all properties are considered insurable, whether located in high risk or safer areas, or whether constructed of wood or less incendiary materials.

Privatizing the INS

The most serious efforts to privatize the Instituto Nacional de Seguros have been exerted in the context of discussions around the Central American Free Trade Agreement (CAFTA) reviewed in the first part of this chapter. Details regarding INS are found in Chapter 12 of the Preliminary Draft on "Financial Services," and in Annex No. III, Article 12.2, insertion 2.

As with Dr. Serrano's (2004) criticism of CCSS privatization under CAFTA, the most authoritative criticism of CAFTA efforts at privatizing the INS comes from "the inside"—from Costa Rica's Association of INS Professionals (APINS). In their letter of February 15, 2005, to Dr. Otón Solis Fallas of the Citizens' Action Party, APINS recognizes the need for structural reforms within the INS, to minimize admitted administration inefficiency, procedural errors, untoward influences, and impunities. Despite such acknowledgements, however, APINS (2005) objects that CAFTA's privatization program on several grounds:

> 1. It obliges Costa Rica to surrender one of its most effective tools for the redistribution of social, political and economic power. As such, at its founding in 1924, it implemented the principles of Catholic social teaching and counteracted the consolidated power of the commercial and landowning elite of the period (APINS).

> 2. The INS provides a service that private industry has proven unable to offer with the same degree of efficiency. This is because insurance by nature is a social service intended to serve all members of society, including the poor whose property is commonly considered uninsurable by private firms who favor "good risks" in their quest to maximize profit. In this connection the APINS (2005) letter quotes Tomas Soley Guell, the father of Costa Rica's state insurance monopoly (*La Prensa*). Writing in 1924, Soley said:

Classical economists use the aphorism: "The state should not do what private industry can." However, *private industry is not able to realize the social function of insurance, but only its mercantile function.* . . Private companies cannot offer services that correspond to the modern concept of insurance, which encompasses the idea of social foresight in all its fullness including considerations of justice and community welfare. Private insurance selects the lucrative parts of risks; in contrast, the State derives from those lucrative parts, by way of compensation, the means for providing insurances of greater social utility, such as is necessary to cover on-the-job injuries, retirements, and pensions (p. 3).

3. INS privatization replaces a state monopoly with social conscience with a private oligopoly concentrated on maximizing profit. Instead of having a single entity controlling insurance within Costa Rica, only four large multinational corporations [AIG (U.S.), ING (Holland), Grupo Generali (Italy), and Grupo Mapfre (Spain)] will most likely use dumping practices to absorb local competition and take over insurance provision within the country (APINS, 2005). Since all these companies are obviously "for profit," and without particular commitment to the overall well-being of Costa Ricans, they will, once again, favor "good risks" and refuse to insure higher risk clients. In fact, 62 percent of the clients of the companies just named are large businesses, 30 percent of whom are banking and financial concerns (APINS).

4. International businesses, like those mentioned in the previous point, generate comparatively little employment and do not contribute greatly to the development of a national insurance infrastructure. They are also largely free from genuine Costa Rican oversight (APINS, 2005). The list of national institutions subsidized by INS income is long and includes the Association of Costa Rican Firefighters, the National Emergency Commission, the Highway Security Council, Supplementary Pensions, and the CCSS itself. Under the CAFTA regime of insurance privatization, such institutions will either be extremely weakened, will disappear, or will have to search elsewhere for replacement funds. The losers in these "technical adjustments," would the less well-off Costa Ricans, whose welfare would be endangered. The APINS (2005) letter reminds Dr. Solis that during Costa Rica's most recent economic crisis, workers continued to be covered fully by their INS policies. This would surely not have been the case under a privatized insurance regime:

Though the Workers Compensation Division suffered losses in recent years, at no time did the Institution stop investing in worker protection, nor were benefits ever trimmed, nor was coverage significantly reduced.[15] On the contrary, the Institution's reserves made it possible to increase social investment and to improve infrastructure. Under private, for profit insurance arrangements, like those proposed (in the CAFTA), the first measure to deal with such crises would be an increase in premium prices in order to balance books, along with a freeze on all investment. If such measure proved inefficacious, the next measure would be to narrow the conditions for policy payments; ultimately there would be recourse to changing insurance law (p. 4).

5. INS privatization represents a loss of Costa Rican national sovereignty. Here the APINS letter agrees with Dr. Serrano's critique of CCSS privatization under CAFTA. The privatization proposals in question fail to honor the principle of reciprocity. That is, Costa Rica's insurance market would be opened unconditionally. This differs from CAFTA arrangements with other countries that negotiated clauses defending their national sovereignty, by, for instance, excluding privatization of insurances connected with social security (APINS). They also negotiated timetables that did not activate till after official treaty approval. Meanwhile, in the United States itself, cross-border insurance sales are restricted to certain products only, and branch insurance companies are expressly forbidden by U.S. law. Such lack of reciprocity and consistency raises fundamental questions about what Costa Rica has bargained for. As the APINS (2005) document puts it:

> Will all the other signatory countries be disposed to assume a universal Workers' Compensation regime following the solidarity model like our own; or, on the contrary, must Costa Rica dismantle its own regime to make it competitive, selective and market-oriented, in order to escape accusations of "discriminatory treatment"? (p. 7)

In the end, the APINS document sees the privatization of INS as a sell-out of a national patrimony. Having been achieved by long years of struggle, development and fine-tuning, it has achieved for Costa Rica a strategic standing similar to petroleum for Mexico and copper for Chile. Both of these countries succeeded in excluding those patrimonies from free-trade agreements with the United States. Costa Rica, it has been argued above, should do the same with its insurance monopoly. Clearly, the purported negative effects of the privatization of the Costa Rican system deserve full and transparent debate (Jimenez, n.d.).

Conclusions

Understanding Costa Rica's "solidarity system" is central to the evaluation of the prospects for the privatization of INS. Not only does the system guarantee that all Costa Ricans, regardless of their financial resources, will have access to occupational injury protection, general health care, automobile, fire and property insurance (including crop indemnities), the system also generates enough surplus to transfer millions of colones to other government entities offering a wide variety of services to Costa Rican citizens. The following table indicates the scope of such transfers.

Table 6.1. Transferencias del Instituto Nacional de Seguros a otras instituciones durante

Aporte	Monto
Fideicomiso Agropecuario	5.523.000,000
Cuerpo de Bomberos	¢5.918.872,328
Utilidades del 2003 al Gobierno	¢500.000,000
Comisión Nacional de Emergencias Ley No. 7914	¢244.620,321
OVSICORI	¢27.180,036
Impuesto de Renta***	¢4.594.355,556
Patente municipal y bienes inmuebles	¢136.613,188
Impuesto de Ventas	¢9.771.784,543
Impuesto sobre la renta (2 percent)	¢505.959,692
Cuota a organismos internacionales Ley No. 3418	¢57.787,436
Consejo de Seguridad Vial Ley No.6324	¢5.081.456,571
Pensiones Complementarias Ley No.7732	¢7.558,207
Cuota patronal I.N.A. Ley No.6868	¢76.079,976
Cuota patronal Asignaciones Familiares Ley No.5662	¢767.766,796
Cuota Patronal I.M.A.S. Ley No.6443	¢70.752,683
Cuota Patronal CCSS Enfermedad, Maternidad e Invalidez Vejez y Muerte	¢2.144.864,485
Cuota Patronal Banco Popular Ley No.5435	¢66.037,788
Aporte Ley de Protección al Trabajador No.7983	¢550.685,268
Aporte Patronal CCSS Ley 7983**	¢1.548.686,807
Aporte SUPEN	¢7.558,207
Diferencia del Cobro Derechos de Circulación	¢153.983,532
Aporte a la Cultura	¢14.939,425
Aporte a la Educación	¢6.226,007
Apoyo al Deporte	¢11.246,982
Apoyo Gubernamental	¢37.708,003
Aporte a la Salud	¢56.931,837

Table 6.1. (continued)

Campañas de Prevención   ¢194.206,263

Total   **¢38.076.861,937**

* Los montos correspondientes a los meses de noviembre y diciembre se
han
  estimado.

** Aporte del SICERE como recaudador.

*** Adelanto del Impuesto de la Renta 2003.

The table indicates that firefighters, farmers, renters of homes, pensioners, expectant mothers, the elderly, sports facilities, emergency services, and others have all benefited from INS collections. With the privatization of the State Insurance Monopoly, such subsidies (at least from the INS source) would stop. The state would be left with the problem of overcoming the shortfall.

With the opening of the insurance market as understood in the proposed CAFTA document, the Costa Rican State also appears to abdicate its legal and even constitutional responsibilities. That is, the section of CAFTA dealing with insurance appears to contradict Article 7 of Law No. 12 of October 30, 1924, the Monopoly Law of the National Institute of Insurance: "The capital acquired by the Institute, as well as its reserves, guarantee especially its insurance operations. These and all the other operations of the Institute remain under the guarantee and full responsibility of the State."

In other words, while favorable treatment of one company over another would render the Costa Rican government in violation of proposed CAFTA treaty obligations, not offering preferential treatment, when judged appropriate by the Costa Rican National Assembly, would apparently constitute a violation of the law which originally established the INS. For that reason, Assembly members would appear to be violating their obligations of office, surrendering their constitutional responsibilities to entities outside the national boundaries.

Henry Mora (2004) indicates the Constitutional responsibilities jeopardized by the CAFTA pact. Costa Rica's National Constitution expressly forbids alteration of the foundations of the established economic order by means of ordinary legislation (2004). The National Constitution also forbids the Legislative or Executive branch of the government to renounce the exercise of the functions that belong to them, and none of these Authorities may delegate the exercise of the functions that are properly theirs. Important for consideration here, these functions include the regulation of investment, both national and foreign (2004).

Apart from legislative and constitutional considerations, the privatization of INS would appear to threaten the universality of coverage currently realized by Costa Rican nationals. In the case of insurance against occupational injury, for example, the fear among privatization's detractors is that worker coverage would deteriorate and remove this important protection. Given the already noted tendency of employers not to insure their workers, even under current law, voluntary coverage in a private system would almost certainly leave many workers uninsured by employers seeking to reduce their costs. Under a private insurance system, the predictable tendency would be to leave the choice to insure workers or not to the voluntary option of company managers and result in even more workers without hazard insurance.

Furthermore, it is fairly certain that private occupational insurance companies would willingly cover low-risk occupations such as office secretaries or classroom teachers against on-the-job injury. Meanwhile, high-risk occupations such as building construction or the manufacture of products utilizing hazardous materials would either be considered too risky or would demand high premiums unaffordable to those typically engaged in such work.

Similar concerns have surfaced about other aspects of INS's potential dismantling. Small farmers would lose protection against crop failure. Older vehicles would be more costly to insure.[16] Homes in high risk areas or those that are constructed below building code standards or of materials considered more flammable would go uninsured.

> . . . in an open market or with the (state) monopoly broken, private companies will seek the "good risks." These will be clients with a great deal of money, with good newer model vehicles, and with concrete houses in secure neighborhoods. Private firms will insure those who are healthy, without inherited illnesses, and who are young.
>
> According to this logic, those without sufficient economic resources, with vehicles of a certain age, who live in wooden houses in high risk neighborhoods, whose health is not good, who suffer from congenital illnesses, diabetes, hypertension, or who are not young, will not be considered "good risks" for private insurance companies. Therefore opening the Monopoly will leave most such people unprotected. Over the more than 80 years of its existence the Monopoly of Insurance has never refused to insure persons on the basis of what they have or what they are. This is because its interest has been merely social and not commercial (Fumero, 2004, p.163).

Finally, the privatization of insurance has historically led to fraud and irresponsibility on the part of many firms involved. When great tragedy strikes, private companies often simply declare themselves bankrupt and unable to meet their obligations. The would-be insured are left without recourse. Alternatively, companies simply leave town in the face of meeting extraordinary payments. This occurred, for instance, following the devastating Managua earthquake of 1972. Following that tragedy, companies left the city in ruins, taking with them their clients' money, while leaving behind everything—typewriters, desks, archives. Similarly, when a severe earthquake in 1991 destroyed a great part of Bocas del Toro in Panama, many private insurers abruptly left the area. Others changed the names of their companies and refused to pay. Meanwhile in Costa Rica, in the adjoining costal city of Limón that also realized terrible damage INS offices stayed open Saturdays and Sundays to pay insurance claims (Fumero, 2004).

The phenomena of irresponsible insurance agencies are not limited to Third World Countries. They are found in the developed world as well. Recently, following Hurricane Andrew in Miami, some private North American companies declared themselves bankrupt in view of the losses they foresaw themselves sustaining. They did this despite the strict controls that exist in the U.S.A. through the Office of Insurance Oversight.

---

1. Any worker opposition within the Caja is significant, since the workforce there is highly organized. Forty-four labor organizations are found within the system. These include unions, associations, solidarity groups, and cooperatives (principally credit unions). Medical doctors, nurses, nurses aides, department directors, paramedics, social workers, dental technicians, anesthesiologists, nutritionists, etc., all have their own unions. Within this system, hospital unions and the National Union of Caja Employees (UNDECA) operate as industrial unions. Among all these organizations, the principal opponents of privatization were UNDECA, the National Association of Nursing Professionals (ANPE), and the Union of Nurses Aides (SINAE) (Salas Picado, 1995).

2. Shiva (2001) elaborates: "Patents give the patent holder the exclusive right to his invention covering the making, rising, exercising, selling, or distribution of the patented article or substance, as well as using and exercising the patented method or process of manufacturing an article or substance" (p. 6).

3. As will be seen presently, this was true also in the United States. On March 28, 1787, the Commonwealth of Pennsylvania awarded John Fitch a patent for the manufacture, use, and navigation of all and every species of steamboat, despite the fact that Scotland's James Watt had invented the steam engine fifteen years earlier, in 1772 (Shiva, 2001).

4, According to U.S. provisions, the clock governing the 20-year span of patents begins ticking the day a patent is applied for. The "patent pending" process usually takes ten or eleven years. CAFTA provisions would have the clock begin ticking the day the patent is granted, thus extending the patent by ten or eleven years (Devandas, 2004). Moreover, amendments to patents, indicating an "error" in the original patent filing (e.g., the exclusion or inclusion of a given formula component) would restart the patent clock, thus, again extending, and perhaps doubling or tripling the life of the patent (Weissman, 2004). Even more importantly, medical patents recognized in the CAFTA would enable patent holders to avoid disclosing product content and testing results. These currently required published data normally relieve producers of generic products from obligations of "rediscovering" a given formula and of replicating the tests required of the product's innovators (Weissman). Instead, all that is required of generic producers is that they supply testing data showing that their products contain the same ingredients as the patented version. The CAFTA would change that arrangement (Devandas). Generic products manufactured after the expiration of a patent would have to be validated by the repetition of the testing process – once again an extremely costly procedure. Cost considerations and lack of testing facilities in many Third World countries would accordingly prohibit them from meeting these new requirements, thus in effect making permanent the originally granted patent, with its attendant higher prices. In this way, the temporary departure from free market theory represented by patents is also perpetuated.

5. According to Salas Picado (1995), the case of Pavas represents the only case in which local communities have not supported the positions of labor organizations relative to privatization.

6. During the late Teens and early Twenties of the last century, the practice of unscrupulous businessmen and others setting fire to their property after insuring it with foreign companies (who, presumably because of the distances involved, operated on good-faith principles) became widespread. Residents of Heredia, for instance, describe a favorite Saturday night pastime – sitting on the city's hills to watch the fires in San Jose. A prominent San Jose businessman is said to have had his enjoyment at a local club interrupted by an urgent telegram from one of his employees asking "When was it that you wanted me to start the fire?" (Jimenez, 2003, p. 2). Such practices bankrupted insurance companies and led to the establishment of Costa Rica's national insurance monopoly under the leadership of Tomas Soley Guell – significantly, the nation's secretary of housing. Apart from his concern about housing's connection with the arson epidemic, Jimenez's thinking was that the reserves produced by the monopoly, then being repatriated to foreign countries, might be kept within Costa Rican borders to help raise standards of living there (Jimenez, 2004a). Establishment of the country's insurance monopoly was seen as Soley's personal triumph (*La Prensa* ,1924). It was immediately recognized as the best insurance company in Central America and even in all of Latin America (La Prensa).

7. The amount of money that would be lost to the Costa Rican economy is indicated by the 2003 earnings of the INS that surpassed the $5 billion figure (Fumero, 2004).

8. In 2003, the State insurance monopoly contributed more than $7 billion to the country's social services (Fumero, 2004).

9. Informational and training programs of these types showed the following results for the year 2003: Owners and workers of 1,236 businesses were trained – a total of 4,067 actual participants and a working population of 415,374 potentially affected. In addition more than 25 different pamphlets and manuals were published. Informational outreach programs were also extended to universities and high schools and were attended by students of the institutions involved (Fumero, 2004).

10. These were attended by 270 businesses, with an average of 137 workers present at each meeting—to the potential benefit of 37,200 total employees. (Fumero, 2004).

11. Under this program the INS-Health Department evaluated labor stations, responded to complaints, investigated serious accidents, and provided consultation and environmental evaluation to businesses concerning physical and chemical agents.

12. For instance, since 1996, all services provided by the INS have been interconnected by the computerized S.I.M.A. (Sistema de Información Medico Administrativo [Medical Administrative Information System]) program. This keeps track of all services offered particular patients who receive medical attention as part of INS health services. This personalized information program records medical consultation summaries, nurses' notes, prescriptions and their results, diagnoses, and other information. The use of SIMA to integrate Costa Rica's entire medical complex has made the system more efficient measured in terms of record keeping and efficacy of services offered to clients. Using SIMA, records of individual patients are immediately available to all with program access, even if a patient must consult, for instance, three separate physicians located in various parts of the country on a single day. In addition, recorded information is more secure and less susceptible to loss. On-line conferences with several medical-service providers can take place with comparative ease, and decisions about medical prescriptions can be made in a more informed way (Fumero, 2004).

13. In 14 separate facilities, INS medical services include among others orthopedics, general medicine, ophthalmology, cardiology, neurosurgery, occupational medicine, internal medicine, minor surgery, urology, gynecology, psychology, psychiatry, dermatology, radiology, and reconstructive surgery, along with services such as pharmacies, infirmaries, transportation, physical therapy, voice therapy, occupational therapy, preventive medicine, and social work. In addition, the INS uses a network of contracted external service providers for special examinations and surgeries, for lab work, for hospital food provision, etc. (Fumero, 2004).

14. Large landowners have lobbied for the privatization of the insurance business (Fumero, 2004). Farmers who cannot pay the high cost of crop insurance might be forced to sell their farms, in the event of unexpected losses (a common occurrence in the agricultural sector). The larger landowners would be in a favorable position to purchase the foreclosed farms and thus increase their holdings and profits.

15. Reasons for the INS shortfall, the APINS letter (2005) notes, were the transfer of 33 percent of the Workers' Compensation reserves to support Cost Rica's national pension plan. Additionally, in September 2001, banana workers employed by Standard Fruit had to be compensated for damages they suffered from use of the pesticide Nemagon. This cost the INS nearly a billion and a half colones. What would have happened, the APINS authors ask, had such an outlay been required of private insurance agencies (2005)?

16. The INS Personnel Union estimates that the dissolution of the State Insurance Monopoly would result in an 876 percent increase in the automobile insurance required of taxi chauffeurs. City buses would be subject to a 166 percent increase (Fumero, 2004).

Chapter 7
Conclusion

Introduction

On the eve of Costa Rica's decision about signing the Central American Free Trade Agreement (CAFTA), many problems relative to the treaty's privatization of key elements of the country's unique social heritage remain unresolved. As a result, the governmental parties to the treaty, as well as the key international agencies involved, have been met with serious, and growing, public opposition to their plans. This study has suggested that with or without the CAFTA, privatization and related economic approaches *can* indeed have an important role to play in adjusting Costa Rica's economy to the realities of globalization. Nonetheless, historical, documentary, and statistical data, as well as the authoritative testimony of individuals centrally involved in the process, indicate that current approaches to privatization are questionable because they do not safeguard the interests of the country's consumers with the same solicitude afforded the companies that would appropriate its material, economic, and social structures and infrastructures.

Furthermore, as indicated in chapter 1, the impact of privatization measures in Costa Rica is evaluated with reference to the specific goals assigned its program by the presidents central to the project, namely Monge, Calderón, and Arias. These goals were outlined in the Legal Project for the Democratization of the Public Sector. In this respect, this study identifies (below) contradictions and inconsistencies among other gaps between their stated goals and their actual delivery.

This final chapter concludes that, for Costa Rican privatization to be effective, certain basic principles and standards must be observed. The final analysis and articulation of those standards and principles is preceded by a brief review of the contents of this study thus far.

Privatization's Meaning and Changing Perceptions

This study attempted to clarify the meaning of privatization. The study saw that even informed analysts on both sides of the debate frequently use the term as though it were an all or nothing unequivocal concept. Too often the question has been framed as though one must either be for privatization or for public owner-ship and administration. Frequently no middle ground is acknowledged. On the one hand, privatization's advocates are often hesitant to acknowledge the short-comings of full cost-recovery privatization of public services and are slow to acknowledge the necessity for partnership with public authorities. On the other hand, public-provision advocates too often blind themselves to the inadequacy of many public services that for decades have borrowed from institutions like the World Bank with no nod to a commercial ethic or apparent concern about im-provement of services. The shortcomings of many public operations must them-selves accept responsibility for prompting privatization initiatives. In either case, the worst part of painting privatization efforts in black and white is that the re-sulting portraiture fails to appreciate the complexity of public-service provision and the potential utility and limits of privatization.

Much of the confusion surrounding the privatization debate is diminished once one realizes that the term's application is not limited to the sale of public assets and services by a government to a private company on the theory that the service will thus be provided more equitably, efficiently, and at a lower cost to the consumer. Instead, this study has broadened the meaning of privatization to include applying market standards and dynamics to the provision of public goods and services. Accordingly, principles of supply and demand, balancing books, minimizing and recovering costs, as well as generating profit are all centralized.

Changed Perceptions

With that understanding in mind, we have seen that such profit-driven principles cannot alone be relied upon to provide public services at fair, equitable prices. This has become increasingly evident to many observers—including World Bank officials. Despite previous unqualified fervor for privatization over the past two and a half decades, the bank's records themselves indicate that its officials have come to realize that privatization is a limited tool for economic and social development. For instance, as of early 2004, the World Bank's official policy on privatization was as follows:

> The WB will continue its model of encouraging private sector participation as a means to improve performance. Financing inefficient public utilities without a clear reform agenda will remain part of the past. **However, reliance on the private sector alone will not be sufficient to guarantee a scaling up of infrastructure** [emphasis

added]. Therefore, the WB will continue to lend in some cases to well-performing public utilities. (Leipziger, 2004)

The emphasized sentence in this statement differs substantially from the Bank's policy on privatization throughout most of the 1990s. Then the Bank almost universally endorsed privatization as the best way to improve government services and strongly encouraged its implementation. Internal peer reviews from the same period indicate a similar shift among World Bank specialists concerning the utility of privatization. For instance, the following questions were asked in a World Bank staff survey in 2003:

> a. Five years ago, how convinced did you personally feel that the new infra-structure sector reform model[1] developed in the 1990s was likely to produce positive results in the kind of sector and countries that you work?

> b. Today, how convinced do you personally feel?

	Convinced			
	Totally	**Partially**	**Neutral**	**Not Very**
Five Years Ago:	35%	55%	5%	5%
Today:	11%	63%	11%	5%

Source: FPSI (Finance Private Sector & Infrastructure, cf. Leipziger) Staff Survey, 2003

The percentage of World Bank specialists who were "totally" convinced that privatization will lead to economic and progress in the Third World dropped from 35 percent to 11 percent. Meanwhile, the percentage of employees who were "not very" convinced of the virtues of privatization increased from 5 percent to 15 percent. The percentage of people who answered "neutral" rose from 5 percent to 11 percent. Lastly, the percentage of people who are only partially convinced that the privatization reform model is effective increased from 55 percent to 63 percent. In other words, the efficacy of privatization plans in general is increasingly called into question, even at the highest levels.

Costa Rica's Historical Context

The same questioning process receives emphasis in particular cases such as Costa Rica's, the focus of this present inquiry. There the country's unique history has for decades set it apart from its neighbors in terms of its comparative social tranquility, its extensive and efficient government services, elevated standard of living, and its educated and organized labor force. Consequently, this study has emphasized the need to consider the unique history of Costa Rica in evaluating privatization's potential there.

Despite the characteristics just noted, it must be emphasized that Costa Rica has never pretended to be a socialist state. On the contrary, and as indicated by Germán Serrano Pinto (2004),[2] Costa Rica has always been highly protective of private investment. Nonetheless, Serrano insists, the country has traditionally boasted a unique sense of social solidarity and citizen responsibility, as well as a high degree of participation in decision-making by the country's labor force. All of these elements have moved the government on various occasions to judiciously intervene in the country's economy when justified for reasons of the common good. Thus as early as 1843 the national administration invested extensively in highway construction for purposes of facilitating the export of coffee. In 1851, the government took over the business of distilling liquor. In the middle of the 19th century, it unsuccessfully attempted to establish control of the country's banking system, with Don Alfredo Gonzalez Flores finally succeeding in setting up the International Bank of Costa Rica by 1915.[3] In the Political Constitution of 1917, the state accepted the obligation of providing for the welfare of the working class in cases of sickness, old age, or accident. By 1924 Costa Rica's state insurance monopoly had been established. In 1928, the government took over provision of electricity production and distribution. By 1931 it established a monopoly of petroleum import and distribution (Serrano).

State intervention reached a turning point with the accession to the Costa Rica's presidency by Dr. Rafael Angel Calderon during the worldwide Great Depression. At that time Calderon announced a new concept of state, which Serrano (2004) calls the "Rule of Social Law"[4] with some welfare state characteristics (p. 10). Calderon described the concept's underlying understanding of State responsibility in the following words,

> it cannot limit its action to administrative tasks pure and simple, nor to permitting the free play of factors which cannot exist nor progress without a precise order from their interaction. Instead, social harmony demands state intervention, antecedent to open competition on the part of great economic forces, in order to obviate the imposition of a few on others, to the detriment of the tranquil development of the collectivity (Serrano, 2004, p. 10).

Here Calderon recognizes the priority of common good, social peace, and harmony over factors such as free markets, their directive signals, and unrestricted competition. Calderon suggests that free competition is inimical to such harmony and ends by imposing the will of the few (presumably members of the entrepreneurial class) on the many—to the latter's great detriment.

By 1942 Calderon's concept had found expression in Article 51 of revisions to the Costa Rican Constitution. The article defines the role of the state as follows: "The state will seek to improve the welfare of the Costa Rican people

. . . organizing and stimulating production as well as the most appropriate distribution of wealth" (Serrano, 2004, p. 11).

Fulfilling this function entailed strictly regulating foreign investment in the country. Even greater control was exercised over the state's banking system, which was entirely nationalized in 1948. According to Serrano, the idea in doing so was that banking transactions were too important to be left in private hands, and that nationalization was necessary to direct the country's savings towards the creation of the ICE.

Following Costa Rica's 1948 Revolution, Calderon's Rule of Social Law was accepted and reaffirmed by President Jose Figueres, whose National Liberation Party (PLN) defined the state's role in these words:

> The state must realize, through its juridical order, all those functions in which its intervention is justified by reason of the common good. . . . Those forms of property must be reserved to the state which entail such great power of dominion that they cannot be left in private hands without prejudice. (Serrano, 2004, p. 11)

Here the criteria for identifying the limits of privatization include, once again, the common good, and the degree of power represented by a given enterprise. To avoid prejudicing the common good, especially powerful enterprises must be controlled by the representatives of the collectivity.[5]

In 1956 Jose Figueres reiterated those sentiments, articulating in the process the "mixed economy" approach that has been increasingly characteristic of Costa Rica's socio-economic organization since the middle of the 19th century.

> It is not fitting that the State involve itself in the affairs of small businesses, depriving their proprietors of the opportunity that belongs to the citizen entrepreneur.. . . . Neither is administration by the Central Government desirable in public enterprises. . . . It is good that those general businesses belong to the nation according to "socialist" criteria. However, they should be decentralized so they might function with "capitalist" agility (Serrano, 2004, p.11).

According to Serrano, Costa Rica eventually went to extremes in socializing its economy. CODESA was a case in point. Realization of such excesses led to a policy reversal beginning in the mid 1970s and to the subsequent dismantlement of the Entrepreneurial State (CODESA) and to the denationalizing of the banking industry around the same period.

Arguments Pro and Con

Costa Rica's history of state intervention has led to the lively debate documented in previous chapters of this study. Arguments advanced in favor of privatization

of diverse elements of Costa Rica's public sector are several and based on a series of beliefs—some well founded, others less so. At a societal level, it is argued
that privatization can more widely and efficiently satisfy the needs of Costa Ricans in key areas. Commercially, privatization adheres to the capitalist axiom
that "more business is better." Accordingly, it is understood that privatization
can promote the proper application of market economies that encourage efficient
allocation, respond quickly to scarcity signals, and promote market development
in the sectors in question. Financially, privatization advocates ask rhetorically,
who can mobilize capital faster and cheaper than the private sector? Ideologi-
cally, privatization promotes the approach that smaller government is preferable
to its alternative. In terms of historical pragmatics, it is believed that in the post-
Cold War world, competent and efficient programs require private participation.

The risks of privatization are also equally well known. Privatization replaces
control by government officials with at least theoretical concern for the common
good, with directorates focused almost exclusively on maximizing return to their
investors. Such replacement tends to marginalize citizens with little or no income—a significant concern especially in the Third World. Thus privatization,
on the one hand, replaces public bureaucracies responsible to their constituencies
with private bureaucracies responsive to their shareholders. On the other hand,
privatization tends to exacerbate economic inequities often by depriving formerly subsidized recipients of goods and services—of essentials such as health
care, retirement resources, and insurance reimbursement. Additionally, as demonstrated in the CAFTA negotiations, privatization schemes are frequently
rushed through the decision-making process with little public input in terms of
genuine debate and referenda. Privatization agreements also tend to ignore the
impacts on eco-systems, again because the companies involved are in the business of making money, not preserving the environment. As noted in the case of
telecommunications in El Salvador and Nicaragua, service actually deteriorated
rather than improved under their privatization programs. At the municipal level,
a loss of local expertise frequently occurs as well when resident employees are
supplanted by foreign nationals working for large private companies. Moreover,
revenue that was being generated by the relevant sectors and reinvested in the
country frequently leaves the country and is deposited into the accounts of large
transnational corporations.[6]

Principles and Guidelines

In view of broadened understandings of privatization's definition, the unique
history of Costa Rica, and the pros and cons of the privatization debate, criteria
of discernment that honor all such elements seem called for. The suggestion here
is that for private capital, ownership, and decision-making to be effective, certain
normative criteria must be respected. Some of these appear to apply to all priva-

tization applications; others are specific to the Costa Rican context just reviewed. The purpose of each, however, is to constitute a framework of effective, democratically accountable public regulation that potentially guarantees fair pricing, equitable access to essential services, and responsible public stewardship. Notwithstanding privatization's potential as a means to improve the provision of goods and services, its overall utility and effectiveness for improving the lives of ordinary people seems limited. Put otherwise, privatization is best understood as one element in a series of measures necessary to achieve such improvement.

In general, the position supported here is that electrical and telecommunications services, health care, social security, and essential insurances should be managed as both social *and* economic goods. More specifically, the spirit of the times and the short-term evidence provided by the resolution of the Cold War indicate that market principles need prioritization in the universal quest to satisfy human need in today's global village. Nevertheless, in keeping with the arguable successes of the traditional solidarity model like that practiced for more than eighty years in Costa Rica, all goods and services presently under the purview of the state should not simply be understood as economic enterprises governed by market dynamics alone. Rather, they should additionally be seen as social goods subject to social criteria such as the common good and universal inclusion, solidarity, the widest possible democratic participation, subsidiarity, transparency, and reciprocity. Consider each of these principles in order.

Maximization of Market

The victory of capitalism in the Cold War on the one hand, and the widening gap between rich and poor on the other, suggest two conclusions. The first is that the freedom to create, produce, compete, and make profit is widely desired by humans in general. The second conclusion, however, is that free competition favors the already strong and usually results in their victories and in growing poverty for those less well-prepared. The latter is evidenced by the burgeoning numbers of those worldwide living on less than $2 per day, by infant mortality rates, life expectancy figures, and statistics on literacy. These figures suggest that the visible hand of government may be necessary to temper the actions of the market's "invisible hand," which is too often negatively experienced by the world's majority. Considerations like these lead to the formulation of an overarching governing principle to regulate the global economy in general and decisions about privatization in particular. The principle is, *as much market as possible and as much central planning as necessary* (to ensure a dignified human life for each and every human being). The parenthetical addition reveals the bias of the author and is intended to remind analysts of an often seemingly-forgotten social purpose of economic activity.

This formulation finds itself in harmony with this chapter's earlier review of Costa Rica's history of state intervention in the country's economy. It is consonant as well with the country's Constitution. As even free-trade critic Henry Mora (2004), has conceded:

> It is clear and incontestable that the Constituent Assembly of 1949 opted for a decentralized or market economy (capitalism) guaranteeing the right of private property, free enterprise, contractual freedom, and the freedom of the labor force. However the Assembly also placed limits on the extent of the market and introduced constitutional principles referring to public intervention in the economy. Clearly, however, these were to be compatible with the economic model the Assembly had adopted. (p. 34)

Mora goes on to provide a short list of public initiatives constitutionally intended to serve the welfare of Costa Rican citizens. With parenthetical references to the relevant constitutional article, these include:

1. Promotion of housing construction when required for social good (Article 65).
2. Facilitation of adequate wealth distribution (Article 50).
3. Organization and stimulation of production (Article 50).
4. Establishment of minimum wages and regulation of the work day (Article 56).
5. Support for and guarantee of citizens' rights to health and to a healthy, ecologically balanced environment (Article 46 & 50).
6. Protection for the unemployed and facilitation of their prompt return to the workforce (Article 72).
7. Prohibition of private monopolies (Article 46).
8. Special protection for women and children in the workplace (Article 71).
9. Establishment of social security (old age, illness, and maternity) as a universal benefit for workers (Article 73).
10. Facilitation of a politics of national solidarity (Article 74).
11. Support and finance of public education (Articles 77 & 78).
12. Creation of public enterprises and autonomous institutions with administrative independence (Articles 188 & 189).
13. Establishment of taxes and national contributions – e.g. taxes on exports and imports (Article 121, Insert 13).
14. Retention of exclusive rights to certain "public goods" such as water and petroleum (Article 121, Insert 14)
15. Promotion of progress in the arts and sciences (Article 121, Insert 18).

In view of such provisions, Mora (2004) questions whether privatization initiatives, especially as formulated in the CAFTA treaty, violate the Costa Rican Constitution. Particularly relevant to his concern is the prohibition of private monopolies, the establishment of social security, the ability to set up public en-

terprises, the freedom to levy taxes and "national contributions," and the state's
retention of exclusive rights to certain "public goods."

Common Good and Universal Inclusion

Here "common good" refers to conditions necessary to ensure the survival and
dignity of all human beings. The suggestion is that, in dealing with matters central to the overall welfare of the body politic (such as health care, on-the-job
injuries, retirement benefits, and insurance of homes and automobiles), sound
economic reasoning and pure market dynamics should be tempered by government regulation assuring access to the services in question. The governmental
program proposed by Costa Rica's Christian Social Unity Party (1990-1994) in
its section entitled "New Strategy: Economic Development with Social Justices,"
is persuasive: it invokes related principles of subsidiarity (see below) and com-
plementarity, and it identifies the common good as determining the limits of privatization:

> The state governs according to the principles of subsidiarity and complementar-
> ity. Subsidiarity should be understood as the state's promotion of intermediate
> organizations that bring about and execute functions ordered towards the com-
> mon good. Complementarity refers to the state's duty to assume to itself, in vir-
> tue of its own competency and for as long as necessary, all those functions
> which the growing complexity of the internal and external social orders make
> impossible, inconvenient, or difficult for private groups to fulfill without dam-
> aging or affecting the principles of common good (Serrano, 2004, p. 13).

By solidarity is meant prioritizing the common good over the benefit of private
individuals. Such understanding of the state's role in Costa Rica is not of recent
origin. Serrano traces it to the middle of the 18th Century. Practically speaking,
regulation of the type just described entails subsidized rates that are fair and reasonable. Such considerations could also extend to electrical and telecommunication services, since these too are essential for inclusion of citizens as genuine
participants in the global economy under requirements reflected in accords such
as the Central American Free Trade Agreement. Similar considerations about
common good and universal inclusion suggest that the indirect effects of privatization measures on society at large be given a decisive role in determining the
swath of privatization measures. Here the phrase "indirect effects" refers to the
loss of jobs in the process of corporate "down-sizing," to resulting increases in
unemployment rates, to the likely loss of security when poverty indices rise and
street crime proliferates, and to the flight of capital from the local economy as
profits are repatriated to the home countries of multinational firms.

Maintenance of Costa Rica's Solidarity Tradition

As indicated throughout this study, Costa Rica's method for keeping essential goods and services available to its citizenry had been its "solidarity model," referenced in the nation's Constitution (Article 74). In the Constitution's words, the relevant mandate is "to procure a permanent policy of national solidarity" (Serrano, 2004, p.117) This arrangement established structures whereby those with greater ability to pay subsidized those with less ability. For more than 80 years, that notion has been employed on both the individual and corporate levels. Thus individuals with more funds have traditionally been expected to pay higher taxes to assist those with lower incomes. Similarly, within particular state institutions, including CODESA, ICE, and Caja/INS, enterprises and branches that experienced greater profitability supported program components with smaller or even negative profit margins. In none of these cases was the main purpose of the state enterprise to generate profit or even necessarily to cover costs or to break even. Instead, the intention was to serve the "common good" referred to in the previous section. This has been true even with CODESA, whose enterprises were intended to provide low-cost goods for social purposes and whose profits were to be recycled into the general fund or earmarked for specific social purposes. The solidarity principle was understood to serve the common good more directly and comprehensively than market dynamics.

Democratic Participation

A country such as Costa Rica, with its proud heritage of exceptionalism relative to other countries in its immediate region, is solicitous not only about its unique social inheritance but about its intensely participatory democracy. This makes local analysts such as Henry Mora suspicious of privatization initiatives (e.g. associated with the CAFTA) that are shielded from public gaze, that limit participation by all affected parties, whose texts remain largely unread, and that are rushed through decision-making processes without submission to public referenda[7]. Mora (2004) writes:

> Today a new transformist ideology following the neo-liberal pattern has validated itself and attempted to impose its vision of the world and its national project on the rest of the population—not by way of dictatorship, mind you, but by recourse to a technical coup d'état (p. 33).

To avoid this imposition from above, Mora calls for transparency in negotiations and strict observance of Costa Rica's constitutional guarantees. Serrano (2004) proposes slowing the privatization process to a ten-year crawl and employing strictly the principles of reciprocity and subsidiarity. By reciprocity he means that all parties must be bound to similar obligations—a characteristic he finds lacking from CAFTA negotiations that have centralized privatization measures.

By subsidiarity, he refers to the principle that keeps decision-making local and refuses to surrender veto power to far-off internationalized boards of directors. Democratic principles would also suggest including representation by all affected citizens into the negotiating process (employees; business owners, small and large; government officials; lawyers; consumers; environmentalists ...).

Environmental Sustainability

It is important that any public program, in any global location, protect the natural environment, which provides the foundation of human existence. This need to preserve the environment is especially important in the case of Costa Rica, whose principal insertion into the global economy at the point of eco-tourism has become so linked to the country's natural endowments. It would seem counterproductive therefore for the country to surrender to outside interests unregulated access to, or ownership or control of, strategic resources such as water, forests, petroleum, minerals, and/or biodiversity (Merino del Rio, 2004).

Evaluation of Privatization Measures in Costa Rica

The primary juridical document for promoting the process of privatization in Costa Rica, known as the Legal Project for the Democratization of the Public Sector, contained the goals assigned to its program. These goals were referenced by the three Costa Rican presidents principally responsible for privatization's advancement.

The goals included (a) identification of and transfer to the private sector those areas of public administration deemed not strategic, non-essential, and non-regulatory; (b) development of a system of incentives necessary for the stimulation of businesses run by ex-public servants, who would in turn offer those very services to the public; (c) determining incentives for already established businesses to generate employment for ex-public servants. The incentives referred to included payment of loans to public servants electing to leave their public posts; contracting with various private organizations, for a determined length of time, for services transferred to the private sector; financing of feasibility studies to that end; credit facilitation; business training for ex-public servants; juridical and technical consulting (Valverde, 1992).

Promises of Universal Benefit

These measures were presented to the people of Costa Rica as benefiting all of the country's social sectors. For instance, as expressed in section 12 of the "Letter of Intent" sent by the Costa Rican government to the International Monetary Fund in 1982 and 1985:

> The government will do everything possible so that the burden of economic adjustment will be distributed equitably. This intention accords with the principle that in current circumstances and for the foreseeable future, market forces should be the principal determining factor of prices, and that administrative controls and subsidies should be limited to a minimum of basic products so as to benefit above all low income groups (quoted by Trejos & Villalobos, 1992, p. 8).

The first sentence in this citation is important, with its claim to equitable burden sharing. It embodies the aspiration often expressed by protagonists of the global economy with its key elements of structural adjustment and privatization. The phrase evokes recollection of the motto of the World Bank itself—cited critically by the winner of the 2001 Nobel Prize in economics, Joseph E. Stiglitz—"Our dream is a world without poverty" (Stiglitz, 2002, p. 23). Such intentionality as found in that motto and Costa Rica's Letter of Intent provide a primary criterion in reviewing the programs promoted by their formulators: Does the program in question share burdens equitably and make provisions to protect the most vulnerable? Does it move closer to the goals of "a world without poverty"?

Neglect of Social Goals

Generally speaking, the achievement of such lofty social goals seems unlikely, and perhaps even inappropriate, in view of the specific measures reviewed in this study. In this connection, it should be recalled that Trejos (1997) indicated a twofold function for the Social State. The first was the facilitation of capital accumulation; the second was the conciliation of social interest for purposes of maintaining domestic tranquility. The implication from the cases studied in preceeding chapters has been that the new privatized-state emphasizes the first objective but largely ignores the second. Again, it is Trejos who makes this point. By minimalizing the state's social function, Trejos submits that Costa Rica's government has abdicated its previously-owned responsibility as the social conscience of the private sector. The consequences for "the social progress of the entire population" have been of critical concern. Costa Rica's traditional social wage has diminished and in some cases nearly disappeared. Work environments have deteriorated, as workers either lost or found threatened their rights to unionize, to bargain collectively, to strike, and to enjoy job security and free time (Trejos). Internal markets serving these same ordinary Costa Ricans have lost their strength, as wealth has been taken out of the country by privatization phenomena such as maquiladoras, free zones, and services of a seemingly unpayable external debt.

Contradictions

According to Trejos (1997), this represents the triumph of a "management perspective" which has eclipsed the perspective, insights, and needs of employees (p. 131). This approach to political-economy, Trejos argues, is contradictory, inconsistent, and limited. It is contradictory because it has sought to diminish a commercial deficit by one-sidedly promoting exports while simultaneously making no significant effort to diminish imports. Money earned in the export sector has been insufficient to meet the demand for the purchase of imports, thus not only failing to shrink but even increasing Costa Rica's commercial deficit (Trejos & Villalobos, 1992).

A second contradiction has been the use of inflationary measures to cure inflation. Here the reference is to currency devaluations, increased taxes on public services, tax exemptions, and incentives, and raised interest rates. Taken together, these measures have diminished government income, increased the fiscal deficit, and caused further inflation (Trejos & Villalobos, 1992).

Finally, in an effort to reduce government spending, social expenditures have been limited to Costa Rica's neediest. However this policy has caused more and more Costa Ricans to fall into the "neediest" category, thus rekindling a tendency towards ever-increasing government spending (Trejos & Villalobos, 1992).

Inconsistencies

The Costa Rican program linked to privatization has been viewed as inconsistent— theoretically, empirically, and historically—by the same critics referenced above. The theory behind privatization's agenda posits that the market should be left free of government intervention. However, keeping the market free while according priority to the export economy has, in Costa Rica's case, required increasingly frequent and extensive government intervention in the marketplace, mostly on behalf of private entrepreneurs (Trejos & Villalobos, 1992). Prioritizing exports is also challenged empirically. There is little hard evidence to show that an export-led economy has increased domestic production or fostered widespread prosperity among citizens in countries where this strategy has been adopted. Finally, the idea is historically inconsistent that opening markets, relying on exports of agricultural products and raw materials (while privatizing government enterprises and services) will cause any country to join the ranks of developed nations. This has been demonstrated recently by Daza and Fernandez

(2004) who point out that South Korea, Taiwan, Hong Kong, and Singapore all practiced highly protectionist measures to develop their economies. Moreover, these "Asian Tigers," in their push for development, relied on expansion of internal markets driven by nationally-owned heavy industry. The same was true of the United States (Daza and Fernandez). As the current study shows, Costa Rica itself can credit much of its "exceptional" status in Central America to public ownership of a wide range of productive means, to government intervention to protect workers, and to policies to allow local industry to develop for the sake of fostering internal markets.

Limited perspective

The Costa Rican program of privatization and market liberalization is counter-productively limited in its thrust. Trejos and Villalobos (1992) contend that such policies cannot lead to economic growth in either the medium or long term. This is because the country's export-led concentration on international trade, though economically stimulating in the short term, tends to render stagnant the country's internal market. Put otherwise, falling salaries along with privatization's downsizing and layoffs inevitably contract the public's purchasing power and demand in general. In a liberalized and privatized economy, the cost of imports predictably outruns income generated by exports. The cost of the former tends to rise consistently. Meanwhile income from exports of agricultural products and raw materials falls consistently. This is a consequence of regional competitors like Costa Rica, Nicaragua, Guatemala, El Salvador, Honduras, and Panama all tending to produce similar products. As a result of such competition, the prices of coffee, sugar, bananas, and beef fall behind those of computers, refrigerators, televisions, and automobiles (Trejos and Villalobos).

Privatizing the Primary and Essential

Some of Costa Rica's privatization measures were contradictory, inconsistent, and limited. Some also went beyond the stipulations of the Legal Project for the Democratization of the Public Sector referenced above. That is, according to influential Costa Rican anti-privatization activists, the measures often exceeded the categories of "secondary," and "non-essential to the nature of the relevant public service." For example the outsourced services of nutrition and food provision for patients, as well as the cleaning and maintenance of facilities are essential to clinics and hospitals. The prompt recovery of patients often depends on these. Similarly, within the Ministry of Public Works and Transportation (MOPT), the services of inspection, design, and construction of streets and highways are viewed as strategic for the achievement of the objectives justifying the very existence of the enterprise. The same has been said for accounting, secretarial and archival services within the Office of Direct Taxation; such operations, arguably, go to the very heart of that office. By the same token, accounting in the Ministry of Housing has also been considered "strategic" (Valverde, 1993).

Inadequate Provisions for Laid-off Workers

Third, the development of incentives to stimulate businesses run by ex-public servants, as well as incentives to established private companies to employ such laid-off workers, proved more sound in theory than in practice. According to a study by Valverde, Trejos, and Mora (1993), 21 percent of the laid-off state workers never found new employment. Many who did find work did so under less stable conditions, with less remuneration and without labor rights they considered essential—such as holidays, Social Security, vacations, etc. Others relocated under this rubric found themselves subjected to much longer, more intense workdays than they had previously; as a result, many soon left their new posts.

Diminished Oversight

Fourth, according to Valverde (1993), the outsourcing of public services as outlined in the General Law for the Concession of Public Works by Contract diminished necessary oversight. Thus, for example, with the loss of experienced workers in the Ministry of Public Works and Transportation (MOPT), dangerous situations developed around the construction and maintenance of ports, highways, bridges, parks, education centers, etc. Such projects were often left without inspectors and other supervisory personnel. Projects were even turned over to privately-owned construction companies before the General Law received approval (Valverde).

Additionally, the user-fee system mandated by the bill led to an undesirable social stratification whereby access to the relevant public services became limited only to those with capacity to pay for the services in question (Valverde, 1993).

Conclusion of Study

The United Nations Declaration of Human Rights asserts that, along with religious and political freedoms, signatory nations are obliged to provide certain essential services to meet the fundamental needs that people commonly require. These include education, transportation, health care, environmental protection, security, the availability of dignified and adequately remunerated work, and sufficient food, housing, and water (UN Universal Declaration of Human Rights,

Articles 25 & 26). This study has set out to examine the increasing pressure to privatize and commodify most public services under the aegis of multinational corporations and global bureaucracies. This review takes place in a context where important actors are concerned that such pressure threatens to undermine the historical role of the state relative to the human rights mentioned. More specifically, those against privatization of electricity, telecommunications, healthcare, social security, and basic insurances in Costa Rica make the added case that the goods and services represented by the provider agencies represent a collective birthright of Costa Ricans within the industrialized global village. The frequently- argued conclusion is that efforts by any agency to monopolize ownership of such essential common-heritage resources should be deemed unacceptable.

Regardless of the conclusion's validity, the reality in the Costa Rican context is that universal access to electricity, telecommunications, healthcare, social security, and basic insurances has been considered the historical heritage of every citizen. Correlatively, the responsibility of assuring universal access has been historically considered the obligation of the Costa Rican government. As evidenced in public opinion polls and large demonstrations against privatization efforts linked to the CAFTA, relatively few in Costa Rica extend to private companies the same degree of faith they invest in their government to assure that every person has access to the goods and services involved. That particular governments have been corrupt, unaccountable, and have often failed to meet their obligations evidently does not mean that the private sector is or would be a better guarantor of rights. On the contrary, the most recent examples of government corruption have been precisely linked to privatization kick-backs rather than to government monopolies as such.

Whether the private sector can play a complementary role in assisting Costa Rica to meet its constitutionally mandated responsibility of providing the services in question is open to thoughtful debate, rather than to blanket, hurriedly considered, once-size-fits-all solutions. This study has proposed that there can indeed be a role for private companies, especially relative to the enterprises grouped under the umbrella of CODESA. The primary concern with solely relying on private ownership and market dynamics for the goods and services provided by ICE and by Caja/INS is that their goods and services belong to a different order—one more closely linked to basic needs such as those signaled in the U.N. Declaration. Market institutions, it has been suggested, respond most effectively to the wants and needs of those with financial resources, while too often disregarding the most basic needs of those who do not have the means to pay. Markets are also distorted by protectionism in the form of patents (for instance of medicines) whose life-spans have the potential for indefinite expansion. Market dynamics are deformed as well by the ability of affluent multinational corporations to "dump" their services on local markets (Serrano, 2004).[8] Thus companies sustain short-term losses in order to drive local competitors into bankruptcy, subsequently recouping losses in the form of higher monopolistic prices. Finally, privatization, especially at the hands of multinationals, encourages a form of capital flight that would likely deprive the Costa Rican economy of the multiplier effect represented by money spent and retained within the local economy.

In the end, and despite the opposition to privatization and commoditization of the goods and services examined here, Costa Rica may rightly determine that it is in its public interest to contract for private operation of some of those enterprises. As recognized by this study, there is sometimes a role for private ownership and markets to play in the management, allocation, and delivery even of electricity, telecommunication services, healthcare, social security, and basic insurances. The submission here has been that such privatization should occur only in the framework of effective, democratically-accountable public regulation that guarantees fair pricing, equitable access, and public stewardship. In the final analysis, Costa Ricans and their elected representatives, not unelected supranational global agencies, must retain veto power over any decisions taken.

---

1. According to two different sources at the World Bank, Infrastructure Sector Reform Model is an alternative term for privatization.

2. Former executive president of the INS, as well as Costa Rica's former minister of Labor and Social Security, Serrano took a leading role in CAFTA negotiations. He reported unfavorably to Costa Rica's president about the treaty's impact on the state's 80-year-old insurance monopoly. Shortly thereafter, he was dismissed from his post (Serrano, 2004).

3. The entire banking system was subsequently nationalized in 1948.

4. "Estado Social de Derecho, si bien con rasgos de Estado Benefactor."

5. Such thinking led to the state purchase of the CNFL in 1968. On May 1st of that year, President Trejos Fernandez of the Social Christian Party announced:

> This year we reached an accord of extreme importance for our country, one that fulfilled and completed the desire of generations of Costa Ricans. I'm referring to the effective achievement by which the production and distribution of energy finally resides in national hands. These negotiations, so delicate by their very nature, had to be carried out with great tact and reached their culmination yesterday precisely with the purchase by ICE of the shares of the Power and Light Company, which for decades resided in the hands of Electric Bond and Share (Serrano, 2004, p. 12).

6. Jose Merino del Rio (2004), ex-deputy of Costa Rica's Legislative Assembly and current coordinator of the Political Action Forum, "Another Costa Rica is Possible, Another World Is Possible," describes what he perceives as the deterioration of Costa Rica's standard of living under neo-liberal policy which centralizes privatization of public services:

Living and working conditions for the majority of Costa Ricans are deteriorating. Neoliberalism has made a few people richer, but it has widened the gap of inequality and has thrust more people into poverty and various forms of exclusion and marginalization. Unemployment has risen, and real salaries have tumbled. Pushing privatization, deregulation, and liberalization to the limit erodes our system of public services and social security; it places in serious danger the future of education, healthcare, pensions; it corners and ruins our small farmers and entrepreneurs; it puts our food security at risk; and it opens the way to the depredation of our environment. It has no real public support as stimulating knowledge, culture, the arts, sports, and healthful recreation for ordinary Costa Ricans. Inequality, discrimination, violence, and poverty hit women especially hard. Situations of abuse and child abandonment are on the increase. Large sectors of our youth neither study nor work. Owning a dignified home has become an impossible dream for tens of thousands of our fellow citizens. A regressive tax system increases public deficits and wounds the neediest (Merino del Rio, 2004, p. 6).

7. A similar reaction to the CAFTA process was vividly articulated and even demonstrated by ex-Costa Rican president Rodrigo Carazo Odio, during a February 21, 2005, lecture to the LASP student group. Carazo loaded a table next to the lectern with three large boxes that each contained stacks of papers. He asked the group what it thought they might be? Carazo proceeded to explain that it was a copy of the CAFTA and that he had to use his influence with the current president and pay the equivalent of $100 to obtain the copy.

8. Former executive president of Costa Rica's National Institute of Insurance describes the practice of insurance dumping on the part of multinational firms:

Dumping practices were very frequent when other markets, like Uruguay's, were opened; there multinational insurance companies financed by significant foreign capital charged ridiculously low premiums in order to position themselves favorably in the market, to establish their niche and thereafter to raise their prices. Such practices harmfully distort the insurance market and can wreak catastrophic effects, including the insolvency of insurance companies (Serrano, 2004, p. 114).

References

Aguilar Bulgarelli, O. (1974). Costa Rica y sus hechos políticos de 1948. *EDUCA*. San José, Costa Rica.

Aguilar Bularelli, O. (1987). Evolución histórica de una democracia. San José, Costa Rica: Editorial UNED.

Aguilar Sánchez, C. (2003). *Los (mal) tratados del libre comercio.* (1st ed). San José, Costa Rica: Editorial DEI.

Aguilar Sánchez, C. (2004). *Reflexiones en torno al Tratado de Libre Comercio entre Estados Unidos y Centroamérica (TLC EU-CA): Razones para el rechazo.* (1st ed). San José, Costa Rica: Editorial DEI.

Ameringer, C. D. (1982). *Democracy in Costa Rica.* New York: Praeger Publishers.

APINS. (2005, February 15). Letter to Dr. Ottón Solís Fallas. *Mimeo*, San José, Costa Rica.

Avrigan, T. (2003, September 9). Economic Policy Institute: On the World Bank and the International Monetary Fund. *Mesoamérica*. Costa Rica.

Baer, W. & Birch, M. H. (1994). *Privatization in Latin America: New roles for the public and private Sectors.* Westport, Conn.: Greenwood Press.

Barry, S. J. (2004, October 15). Rodríguez expected back soon. *The Tico Times*, pp. 1, 8-9 (San José, Costa Rica).

Bell, J. P. (1971). *Crisis in Costa Rica: The 1948 revolution.* Austin: University of Texas Press.

Biehl, J. (1988, Junio 6). No me sentí extranjero en Costa Rica. *La Nación.* Costa Rica.

Biesanz, R. (1988). *The Costa Ricans.* Englewood Cliffs, N.J.: Prentice-Hall.

Birch, M. H. & Haar, J. (2000). *The impact of privatization in the Americas.* Coral Gables, Fla.: University of Miami: North-South Center Press.

Bird, Leonard. (1984). *Costa Rica: The unarmed democracy.* London: Sheppard Press.

Boeker, P. H. (1993). *Latin America's turnaround:Privatization, foreign investment, and growth.* San Francisco, Calif: Institute for Contemporary Studies.

Bonilla, H. H. (1975). *Figueres and Costa Rica: An unauthorized political biography.* San José, Costa Rica: Editorial Texto Limitada.

Booth, J. A. (1987). Representative constitutional democracy. In G.W. Greenfield, *Latin American labor unions.* New York: Greenwood Press.

Booth, J. A. (1989). Costa Rica: The roots of democratic stability. In Democracy in developing countries, Latin America (pp. 386-422). Boulder, Colo: Lynne Rienner Publishers, Inc.

Booth, J. A. & Walker, T. W. (1989). *Understanding Central America.* Boulder, Colo: Westview Press.

Brenes Castillo, M. E. (1978). Matina, bastión del contrabando en Costa Rica. San José, Costa Rica: Anvario de Estudios Centroamericanos.

Brooks, S. (1999, May). Liars, filibusters and the future of ICE. *Mesoamérica*. Costa Rica, Vol. 18, Number 5.

Burtless, G., Lawrence, R. Z., Litan, R. E., Shapiro, R. J. (1998). Globaphobia: Confronting fears about open trade. Washington, D.C.: The Brookings Institution Press.

Busey, J. L. (1962). Notes on Costa Rican democracy. Boulder, Colo.: University of Colorado Press.

Canache, A. (2001, June). Congress paralyzed. *Mesoamérica,* Vol. 19, Number 6. Costa Rica.

Caravajal, M. E. (1988, February 12). Bank tries to calm panic. *Tico Times*. Costa Rica.

Cardoso, C. F. S. (1973). La formación de la hacienda cafetalera en Costa Rica (Siglo XIX). *Estudios Sociales Centroamericanos*. Vol. 6, pp. 22-50. Costa Rica.

Cardoso, F. & Faletto, E. (1979). Dependency and development in Latin America. Berkeley, Calif: University of California Press.

Castro, S. (2004). Privatization of the land and agrarian conflict. In S. Palmer and I. Molina, (Eds). *The Costa Rica Reader: History, Culture, Politics*. Durham, N.C.: Duke University Press.

CECADE. (1988, enero). Propuesta de privatización, reestructuración en la C.C.S.S. San José, Costa Rica: Avance de Investigación.

Cerdas Cruz, R. (1975). La crisis de la democracia liberal en Costa Rica: Interpretación y perspectiva (2nd ed.). San José, Costa Rica: Editorial Universitaria Centro-Americana.

Cespedes, V. H. (1983). *Costa Rica: Problemas económicos para la década del los 80s.* San José, Costa Rica: Editorial Studium.

Chenery, H. (1974). *Redistribution with growth*. London: Oxford University Press.

Connolly, M. & Gonzalez-Vega, C. (Eds.). (1987). *Economic reform and stabilization in Latin America*. New York: Praeger.

Conroy, M. E. Murray, D. L., Rosset, P. M. (1996). *A cautionary tale: Failed U. S. development policy in Central America*. Boulder, Colo.: Lynne Rienner Publishers.

Daza E. & Fernández, R. (2004, Mayo-Junio). Nos recetan lo que no hicieron: protección inversión extranjera y exportaciones y su papel en el desarrollo. *Pasos*, 113, pp.17-25 (San José, Costa Rica).

Dengo Obregón, J. M. et al. (1997). Recursos naturales: En la Costa Rica del año 2000. San José, Costa Rica: Ministerio de Cultura.

Devandas, M. (2004). El derecho universal de la población a los medicamentos. In C. Aguilar Sánchez (Ed.) *Reflexiones en Torno al Tratado de Libre Comercio entre Estados Unidos Y Centroamérica (TLC EU-CA) Razones para el Rechazo, p*p. 101-109. San José, Costa Rica: Colección Universitaria.

Diamond, L., Linz, J.L., Lipset, S. M. (Eds.). (1989). *Democracy in developing countries: Latin America* (Vol. 4). Boulder, Colo.: Lynne Rienner Publishers.

Dierckxsens, W. (2000). *The limits of capitalism: An approach to globalization without neoliberalism*. London: St. Martin's Press, Inc..

Dirección de Mercadeo Corporativo y Relaciones Públicas del ICE. (2003, Mayo-Junio). *Impactos y experiencias de las privatizaciones en los sectores de telecomunicaciones y energía en el mundo*. San José, Costa Rica.

Doryan Garrón, E. (1990). De la abolición del ejército al premio nobel de la paz. San José, Costa Rica: Universidad de Costa Rica.

Duchrow, U. & Hinkelammert. (2004). *Property for people, not for profit: Alternatives to the global tyranny of capital.* New York: Zed Books.

Duran, O., Acosta, C., Mata, D. (1991). *Privatización de los servicios de salud ¿una alternativa para la participación popular?* Licénciate thesis in sociology, University of Costa Rica.

Dyer, R. (1988, February). Audit memos charge AID favoritism here. *Tico Times.* Costa Rica.

Echandi Gurdian, M. L. (1996). *La estructura y las potestades del Estado Social de Derecho.* San José: Editorial Universidad de Costa Rica.

Edwards, B. (2003, Jan-Feb.). IDB plan to sell the public sector: The cure or the ill? *NACLA Report on the Americas,* Vol. XXXVI, No. 4, pp. 13-19.

Edelman, M. (1989, September). *A rural protest against economic adjustment in northwestern Costa Rica.* San Juan, Puerto Rico: Latin American Studies Association:

Engelhard, P. (1996). *L'Homme mondial: les societes humaines peuvent-elles survivre?* Paris: Arlea.

Facio, R. (1972). Estudio sobre economía Costarricense. San José, Costa Rica: Editorial de Costa Rica.

Feldstein, M. (1997, August). The case for privatization. *Foreign Affairs.*

Fernández Pinto, R. (1976, abril). Estabilidad y subdesarrollo: Un análisis preliminar de la burocracia en Costa Rica. *Revista de Ciencias Sociales:* UCR, No. 11. Costa Rica.

Ferranti, D. de. (2004). *Inequality in Latin America: breaking with history?* Washington, D.C.World Bank Latin American and Caribbean Studies.

Fields, G.S. (1986, February). Employment and growth in Costa Rica. Washington D.C.: Agency for International Development. Unpublished report.

Figueres Ferrer, J. (1956). Los problemas de la paz y de la guerra: Discurso pronunciado en la reunión de presidente de América. Presentado en Panamá, el 22 de julio del 1956. San José, Costa Rica.

Foster, J. & Sen A. (1997). *On economic inequality.* Oxford: Clarendon Press.

Franco, E. & Sojo, C. (1992). *Gobierno, empresarios y políticas de ajuste.* (1ª ed) San José: FLACSO.

Fuentes-Belgrave, L. (2001, Marzo). Las tres semanas del 'Combo.' *Se Mueve.* San José, Costa Rica.

Fumero, G. (2004). Costa Rica en el marco del Tratado de Libre Comercio Estados Unidos-Centroamérica y sus consecuencias en el área de las telecomunicaciones. In C. Aguilar Sánchez (Ed.) *Reflexiones en Torno al Tratado de Libre Comercio entre Estados Unidos Y Centroamérica (TLC EU-CA) Razones para el Rechazo.* San José, Costa Rica: Colección Universitaria.

Garita, L. (1981). El proceso de burocratización del Estado Costarricense. *Ciencias Económicas I,* Vol. 1. San José, Costa Rica.

Glade, W. & Corona, R. (1996). *Bigger economies, smaller governments: Privatization in Latin America.* Boulder, Colo: Westview Press.

Geiger, E. P. (1991). *Privatización y política económica.* San José, Costa Rica: ANFE.

George, S. (1988). *A fate worse than debt: The world financial crisis and the poor.* New York: Grove Wedenfeld.

González Flores, L. F. (1974). El desenvolvimiento histórico del desarrollo del café en Costa Rica y su influencia en la cultura nacional. *Revista de Costa Rica.* Vol. 5, pp. 97-112. Costa Rica.

Gonzalez Vega, C. (1984a). *Growth and equity: Changes in income distribution in Costa Rica.* New York: United Nations.

Gonzalez Vega, C. (1984b). Fear of adjusting: The social cost of economic policies in Costa Rica in the 1970s. In D. Schulz & D. Graham (Eds.), *Revolution and counterrevolution in Central America and the Caribbean.* Boulder, Colo: Westview Press.

Guerra, T. (1987). José Figueres una vida por la justicia social. Heredia, Costa Rica: CEDAL.

Hale, V. (2004, Dec. 6). Creating more paths to hope. *Newsweek*, p. 80.

Hall, C. (1985). *Costa Rica, a geographical interpretation in historical perspective.* Syracuse University: Dellplain Latin American Studies, Department of Geography.

Haider, A. K. (1993, April-May). Democracy, markets and structural adjustment. *Xerox.* University of Denver.

Hinkelammert, F. J. (1988) La deuda externa de América Latina: el automatismo de la deuda. San José, Costa Rica: Departamento Ecuménico de Investigaciones.

Hinkelammert, F. J. (1999) El huracán de la globalización. San José, Costa Rica: Departamento Ecuménico de Investigaciones.

Hinkelammert, F. J. (2003a). *El asalto al poder mundial y la violencia sagrada del imperio.* (1st ed). San José, Costa Rica.

Hinkelammert, F. J. (2003b). El sujeto y la ley. San José, Costa Rica: Departamento Ecuménico de Investigaciones.

Hippler, J. (1995) *The Democratisation of disempowerment: The problem of democracy in the Third World.* London: Pluto Press.

Holland, J. & Henriot, P. (1983). *Social analysis: Linking faith and justice.* New York: Orbis Books.

Honey, M.(1994). *Hostile acts: U.S. policy in Costa Rica in the 1980s.* Gainesville: University of Florida Press.

I. G. Patel. (1993). Limits of the current consensus on development. World Bank Annual Conference.

ICE Relaciones Públicas. (1988a). *El ABC del ICE.* San José, CR.

ICE Relaciones Públicas. (1988b). *Ice Electricidad y Telecomunicaciones.* San José, CR.

Jameson, F. & Miyoski, M. (1998). *The cultures of Globalization.* Durham and London: Duke University Press.

Jiménez Sandí, M. J. (1999, Oct-Dec.) Historia del Segural Comercial en Costa Rica. Folleto catálogo exposición INS 75 aniversario. San Jose, Costa Rica: Museo de Jade Marco Fidel Tristan.

Jiménez Sandí, M. J. (2003, May 30). La ley de seguros en la historia de Costa Rica. *Mimeo*, San José, Costa Rica.

Jiménez Sandí, M. J. (2004, September 1). Setiembre (sic) de 1924. *Mimeo*, San José, Costa Rica.

Jiménez Sandí, M. J. (2004, Dec. 21). 1925 Un año de acontecimientos. *Mimeo*, San José, Costa Rica.

Jiménez Solé, R. (no date). Los seguros en el TLC: urgente transparencia y necesaria información. *Mimeo*, San José, Costa Rica.

Klarén, P. F. & Bossert, T. J. (1986). *Promise of development: Theories of change in Latin America.* Boulder, Colo.: Westview Press, Inc.

Korten, A. (1997). *Ajuste estructural en Costa Rica: Una medida amarga.* (1st ed). San José, Costa Rica: DEI.

Korten, D. C. (2001). *When corportations rule the world.* Bloomfield, Conn: Kumarian Press.

Lawton, J. A. (1995). *Privatization amidst poverty: Contemporary challenges in Latin American political economy.* Boulder, Colo.: Lynne Rienner Publishers.

La Prensa. (1924, Oct. 28). El triunfo del Secretario de Hacienda en el monopolio de seguros (San José, Costa Rica).

Lack, S., Laurent, K., Espinoza, C., Christiansen, A., & Calvert, D. (1989). Final evaluation report: Agricultural crop diversification/export promotion cross-cutting evaluation. Washington D.C.: Experience, Inc.

Lara, S. (1995). *Costa Rica: The essential guide to its politics, economy, society and environment.* Albuquerque, N.M.: Interhemispheric Resource Center.

Latinamerica Press. (1999, Sept. 27). Death of a theory. Vol. 31, No. 35. San José, Costa Rica.

Leipziger, D. (2004, Oct.). The privatization debate: Finance private sector and infrastructura. *World Bank Commentary.*

Lizano, E. (1990). *Crisis económica y ajuste estructural.* (1st ed). San José, Costa Rica: EUNED.

Mander, J. & Goldsmith, E. (Eds.). (1996). *The case against the global economy: And for a turn towards the local.* San Francisco: Sierra Club Books.

Manzetti, L. (1999). *Privatization: South American Style.* London: Oxford University Press.

Melendez, C. (1985a). Bosquejo para una historia social costarricense antes de la independencia. In V. de la Cruz et al, *Las instituciones costarricenses del siglo XIX.* San Jose, Costa Rica: Editorial C.R.

Melendez, C. (1985b). *Historia de Costa Rica.* San José, Costa Rica: EUNED.

Merino de Rio, J. (2004). Otra Costa Rica es possible. *Foro de Accion Politica.* San José, Costa Rica:.

Mesa-Lago, C. (1994). *Changing social security in Latin America: toward alleviating the social costs of economic reform.* Boulder, Colo.: Lynne Rienner Publishers, Inc.

Mesoamérica. (1997, July). San José, Costa Rica: Institute for Central American Studies.

MIDEPLAN. (1987). *Traslado de servicios del sector público al sector privado.* San José, Costa Rica.

MIDEPLAN. (1998). *Principales indicadores de Costa Rica.* San José, Costa Rica.

MIDEPLAN, Comisión Técnica (1985). Guía de acción para transferir servicios estatales a la actividad privada. San José, Costa Rica.

MIDEPLAN, Comisión Técnica. (1987, May). Dirección de racionalización del estado. San José, Costa Rica.

Monge Alfaro, C. (1976). *Historia de Costa Rica* (14th ed.). San José: Trejos.

Mora, H. (2004). El Tratado de Libre Comercio, la economía y la constitución política. In C. Aguilar Sánchez (Ed.) *Reflexiones en Torno al Tratado de Libre Comercio entre Estados Unidos Y Centroamérica (TLC EU-CA) Razones para el Rechazo.* San José, Costa Rica: Colección Universitaria. Pp. 31-53.

Mora Jiménez, H. (2004, Agosto). *Para oponernos al TLC entre Centroamérica y Estados Unidos.* San José, Costa Rica: Editorial EUNA.

NACLA. (2003, Jan/Feb.). Privatization and its discontents. *NACLA Report on the Americas.* Volume XXXVI, No. 3.

Nelson, J.M. (1989). Crisis management, economic reform, and Costa Rican democracy. In B. Stallings & R. Kaufman (Eds.), *Debt and democracy in Latin America.* Boulder, Colo.: Westview Press.

Newton, J., Lieberson, J., Sines, R., Miller, D., Fox, J., Zuvekas, C. (1988). *The effectiveness and economic development impact of policy-based cash transfer programs: The case of Costa Rica.* (A.I.D. Evaluation Special Study No. 57). Washington D.C.: U.S. Agency for International Development.

OFIPLAN. (1982). *Evolución socioeconómica de Costa Rica 1950-1980. San José:* EUNED.

Palma, D. (1980). El estado y la desmovilización social en Costa Rica. *Estudios Sociales Centroamericanos* 27. San José, Costa Rica.

Palmer, S. & Molina, I. (2004). *The Costa Rica reader: history, culture, politics.* Durham and London: Duke University Press.

Peeler, J. A. (1985). *Latin American democracies: Columbia, Costa Rica, Venezuela.* Chapel Hill: University of North Carolina Press.

Perez-Brignoli, H. (1989). *A brief history of Central America.* Berkeley: University of California Press.

Ramamurti, R. (1996). *Privatizing monopolies: Lessons from the telecommunications and transport sectors in Latin American.* Baltimore and London: The Johns Hopkins University Press.

Ramanadham, V. V. (1989). *Privatization in developing countries.* London; New York: Routledge Books.

Rapaport, A.I. (1978). Effective protection rates in Central America. In W.R. Cline & E. Delgado (Eds.), *Economic Integration in Central America.* Washinton D.C.: Brookings Institution.

Reuben, S. (1982). *Capitalismo y crisis económica en Costa Rica: treinta años de desarrollo.* San José: Editorial Porvenir.

Rinehart, R. (1984). Historical setting. In Nelson, H.D. (Ed), *Costa Rica, a country study.* Washington, D.C.: Foreign Area Studies.

Rivage-Seul, D. M & Rivage-Seul, M. K. (1995). *A kinder and gentler tyranny: illusions of a new world order.* Westport, Conn.: Praeger.

Rivera, E. (1982). *El fondo monetario internacional y Costa Rica (1978-1982).* San José, Costa Rica: DEI.

Robinson, E. (2004, May 2). Latin America told to temper market economics. *The Washington Post.*

Rogers, T. (2000, May). Popular democracy in Costa Rica: A threat to neoliberalism? *Mesoamérica,* Vol. 19, Number 5, pp. 9-10.

Rogozinski, J. (1998). High price for change: Privatization in Mexico. *Inter-American Development Bank.*

Romero, J. E. (1982). *La Social Democracia en Costa Rica.* (2nd ed). San José, Costa Rica: EUNED.

Sáenz Pacheco, C. J. (1969). Population growth, economic progress and opportunities on the land: The case of Costa Rica. (Doctoral dissertation, University of Wisconsin).

Salas Picado, D. (1995). *Ajuste, política económica y privatización: La incidencia de los trabajadores en esta política, 1987-1988.* Heredia, Costa Rica: Universidad Nacional.

Salazar, J. M. (1979). *Política y reforma en Costa Rica 1914-1958.* San José: Editorial Porvenir.

Salazar, J. M. (1986). Efectos sociales de la crisis económica y las consecuencias para la política social. San José, Costa Rica: Universidad de Costa Rica, Centro de Investigaciones Históricas.

Sanders, S. W. (1986). The Costa Rican laboratory. New York: *The Twentieth Century Fund, Inc.*

Serrano Pinto, G. (2004). *El TLC y los seguros.* (1st ed). San José, Costa Rica: G. Serrano P.

Shallat, L. (1989). AID and the decret parallel state. In Marc Edelman and Joanne Kenan (Eds.), *The Costa Rican Reader*. New York: Grove Press.

Schamis, H. E. (2002) *Re-forming the state: The politics of privatization in Latin America and Europe*. Ann Arbor, Mich.: The University of Michigan Press.

Schulz, D. E., & Graham, D. H. (Eds.) (1984). *Revolution and counterrevolution in Central American and the Caribbean*. Boulder & London: Westview Press.

Shanafelt, A. (2000, December). Miners laid off in Guanacaste. *Mesoamerica*, Vol. 19, Number 12, pp. 6-8 (Costa Rica).

Shiva, V. (2001). *Patents: Myths and reality*. New Delhi, India: Penguin Books.

Sen, A. (1997). *On economic equality*. Oxford: Clarendon Press.

Stallings, B. & Kaufman, R. (1989). *Debt and democracy in Latin America*. Boulder, Colo.: Westview Press, Inc.

Stiglitz, J. E. (2002). *Globalization and its discontents*. New York: Norton & Company.

Stone, S. (1975). La dinastía de los conquistadores. San José, Costa Rica: Editorial Universitaria Centroamericana.

Sunkel, O. & Paz, P. (1973). El subdesarrollo Latinoamericano y la teoría del desarrollo. México, D.F.: Siglo XXI.

Trejos, J. D. (1985). Costa Rica: Economic crisis and public policy, 1974-84. Latin American and Caribbean Center, Occasional Papers Series, No. 11. Miami: Florida International University.

Trejos, M. E. (1997). *Relaciones laborales y reestructuración del estado en Costa Rica*. (1ª ed). Editorial Fundación UNA. Heredia, Costa Rica.

Trejos, M. E. & Valverde, J. M. (1995). *Las organizaciones del magisterio frente al ajuste*. San José, Costa Rica: FLACSO.

Trejos, M. E. & Villalobos, R. (1992, September). Lo aparente y lo oculto del ajuste estructural. Heredia, Costa Rica: National University School of Economics.

UCID. (1981). De los empresarios politicos a los políticos empresarios. Heredia: Oficina de Publicaciones.

Unión del Personal Del Instituto Nacional de Seguros. (2004). El monopolio de los seguros y el seguro: parte importante de la seguridad social costarricense. In C. Aguilar Sánchez (Ed.) Reflexiones en Torno al Tratado de Libre Comercio entre Estados Unidos Y Centroamérica (TLC EU-CA) Razones para el Rechazo. San José, Costa Rica: Colección Universitaria. Pp. 153-71

USAID. (May 1990) Promoting trade and investment in constrained environments: A.I.D. Experience in Latin America and the Caribbean. Report prepared by The Development Economics Group of Louis Berger International, Inc. U.S. Agency for International Development Evaulation Special Study No. 69.

Valverde J. M. (1993). *Proceso de privatización en Costa Rica. . . y la respuesta sindical?* San José, Costa Rica: ASEPROLA.

Valverde, J. M., Trejos, M. E., Mora, M. (1992). El ajuste de la política social: una nueva estrategia de gobernabilidad. Informe final de Investigación. San José, Costa Rica: CLACSO-IIS.

Valverde, J. M., Trejos, M. E., Mora, M. (1993). La movilidad laboral al descubierto. San José, Costa Rica: ANEP-ASEPROLA.

Vargas S., & Paulino, L. (Eds.) (1990). *Crisis económica y ajuste Estructural* (San José, Costa Rica).

Vega, M. (1982). *El estado Costarricense de 1974 a 1978: CODESA y la fracción industrial*. San José, Costa Rica: Editoria Hay.

Vega Carballo, J. L. (1980). *Estado y dominación social en Costa Rica*. San José, Costa Rica: Instituto de Investigaciones Sociales, Facultad de Ciencias Sociales, Universidad de Costa Rica.

Vega Carballo, J. L. (1982). Poder político y democracia en Costa Rica. *Editorial Porvenir*. San Jose, Costa Rica.

Vega Carballo, J. L. (1990). Political parties, political systems and democracy. San Jose: Editorial Universidad de Costa Rica.

Vega Carballo, J.L. (1982). Hacia una interpretación del desarrollo costarricense: Ensayo sociológico. Editorial. *El Porvenir*. San José.

Vega González, C. & Camacho Mejía, E. (1990a). *Políticas económicas en Costa Rica Tomo I*. San José, Costa Rica: Academia de Centroamérica.

Vega González, C. & Camacho Mejía, E. (1990b). *Políticas económicas en Costa Rica Tomo II*. San José, Costa Rica: Academia de Centroamérica.

Vega González, C. & Camacho Mejía, E. (1990c). *Políticas económicas en Costa Rica Tomo III*. San José, Costa Rica: Academia de Centroamérica.

Vernon, R. (1988). The promise of privatization. New York: Council on Foreign Relations, Inc.

Vickers, J. & Yarrow, G. (1988). *Privatization: An Economic Analysis*. Boston: Massachusetts Institute of Technology.

Weissman, R. (2004). Morir por falta de medicamentos: Repercusiones del CAFTA sobre el acceso a los medicamentos esenciales. In C. Aguilar Sánchez (Ed.) *Reflexiones en Torno al Tratado de Libre Comercio entre Estados Unidos Y Centro-américa (TLC EU-CA) Razones para el Rechazo*. San José, Costa Rica: Colección Universitaria. Pp.111-120.

Wiarda, H. J. (1985). The Problem of ethnocentrism in the study of political development: Implications for foreign assistance programs. Washington DC: American Enterprise Institute for Public Policy Research.

Willing, R. D. (1993). Public versus regulated private enterprise. World Bank Annual Conference.

Wilson, B. (1990). Neo-Liberals, Social Democrats, and economic crises: The cases of Costa Rica and Jamaica. St. Louis: Washington University.

Wolkoff, L. (2000, April). Energy bill controversy: The final straw. *Mesoamerica*, Vol.19, Number 4, pp. 1-3. Costa Rica.

World Bank. (1995). Bureaucrats in business: The economics and politics of government ownership. New York: Oxford University Press.

Index

45
FSLN, 8
FTAA, 94
GATT, 110
General Law, 13, 143
Generation of '48, 63
Generation of '89, 35, 37, 41
gold, 22, 28
Gonzalez Flores, Alfredo, 39-40, 132
government administration, 15
Guardia Civil, 48
Guardia Gutierrez, Tomas, 30, 32-33, 37-38, 41-42
Guatemala, 11-12, 23-26, 44-45, 78, 96-97, 142
guilds, 34
health care, 34, 104-05, 109-10, 115-16, 118-20, 123, 134-35, 137, 143
health care and social security, 15, 17
Heredia, 26-27, 31, 85, 128
Honduras, 26, 28, 30, 97, 142
Hundred Days Plan, 105
ICE Combo Bill, 91-92
ICE, 14, 16, 18, 78, 81-99, 144-45
ICELEC, 91-92, 94
ICETEL, 91-92
import subsitution, 2, 3, 16, 55, 100
Inabensa, 99
indispensible public services, 14
INS, 18, 103, 107, 117-18, 120-23, 125
International Monetary Fund, 5, 11, 68-69, 72, 139
IPR, 115
ISI, 55-57, 65
Junta Directiva, 84
Junta Fundadora, 45
Keith, Minor, 33
Kennedy, John F., 73
La Nacion, 94
Labor Union Front, 87
Law No. 12, 117, 125
Law No. 17, 104
Law No. 449, 83
liberal democracy, 34
maintenance of solidarity, 137
maquiladora, 12, 140
marchamo, 120

maximization of market, 135
Meiggs, John, 33
meseta central, 23, 27-28, l25
MIDEPLAN, 12, 105
Monge, Luis Alberto, 11, 12, 18, 51, 68-69, 73, 79, 105-06, 129
Mora Fernandez, Juan, 28
Mora, Henry, 136, 138, 143
Mora, Juan Rafael, 31-32
Mora Porras, Juan Rafael, 30-32, 133
Mora, Valerder, 45
mutual-aid societies, 34
NAFTA, 94
National Union Party, 37
National Republican Party, 37, 41-42
Nicaragua, 23, 25-28, 30, 40-41, 45, 48-49, 66, 78-79, 97, 134, 142
Oduber, Daniel, 9, 16, 59, 63-66
oil crisis, 3-5
Pacheco, Abel , 51, 99
parallel state, 72-75, 77-78
patents, 10, 110-115, 127-28, 144
Pavas, 106-07, 116
Picado, 43-45
Popular Socialist Alliance, 52
Prieto, Marcelo, 66
privatization forms, 8
RACSA, 91
railroad, 10, 33-34, 48
Reagan, Ronald, 4, 11, 73
Republican Party, 37-38, 41, 43
Rodrigo Carazo, 54
Rodriguez, Miguel Angel, 91, 93-95, 99
Rodriguez Zeledon, Jose Juaquin, 36
Roosevelt, Franklin 4, 43
San Jose, 31, 85, 94, 99, 128
Sandinista, 11, 12
Santamaria, Juan, 30
Second Republic, 37-37, 42, 45, 47, 49, 54, 56, 58, 83, 99
Serrano Pinto, German, 107-09, 121, 123, 132-33, 137-38
small farms, 23
social state, 1-4, 8-10, 13-14, 18, 140
socialism, 1, 4, 9, 112
solidarity model, 99, 100, 103, 123

About the Author

Anthony B. Chamberlain is director of the Council for Christian Colleges and Universities' Latin American Studies Program. (The CCCU is a higher education association of 176 member and affiliate colleges and universities from 24 countries.) The author has lived and worked in the Third World for over 20 years, the last 15 in Costa Rica. He has had the opportunity to interact personally with numerous Central American presidents, cabinet level officials, and members of their National Assemblies. This has taken place in an experiential learning context which intends to assist North American university students in gaining a deeper respect for and appreciation of authentic Latin American perspectives.

Chamberlain received his Ph.D. from the University of Maryland, College Park, in political economy and Third World development.

www.ingramcontent.com/pod-product-compliance
Lightning Source LLC
Chambersburg PA
CBHW021819270326
41932CB00007B/252